JOY OF LIVING BIBLE STUDY SERIES

COURAGE TO CONQUER
Studies in Daniel

Life-Related for Personal and Group Study
DORIS W. GREIG

GL
Regal Books
A Division of GL Publications
Ventura, California, U.S.A.

Published by Regal Books
A Division of GL Publications
Ventura, California 93006
Printed in U.S.A.

Library of Congress Cataloging-in-Publication Data:
Greig, Doris W., 1926-
    Courage to conquer : studies in Daniel / Doris W. Greig.
        p.   cm.
    ISBN 0-8307-1285-2
    1. Bible. O.T. Daniel—Study. I. Title.
BS1555.5.G74 1988
224'.5'0076-dc19   88-4398
                                                                                CIP

1 2 3 4 5 6 7 8 9 10 / 91 90 89 88

Rights for publishing this book in other languages are contracted by Gospel Literature International (GLINT) foundation. GLINT also provides technical help for the adaptation, translation, and publishing of Bible study resources and books in scores of languages worldwide. For further information, contact GLINT, Post Office Box 488, Rosemead, California, 91770, U.S.A., or the publisher.

SPECIAL BENEFIT

This book has been conveniently hole-punched and perforated for easy tearout and insertion in a 6″ × 9½″ looseleaf notebook:

- Bible study pages lie flat in your notebook for ease of writing as you study.

- Additional notebook paper can be inserted for journaling or more extensive notes and other relevant information.

- Additional studies in the Joy of Living Series can be inserted, along with your personal notes, and tabbed to help you build your Bible study file for easy, future reference.

CONTENTS

INTRODUCTION

In a world filled with threats of famine, nuclear war and seemingly incurable plagues like AIDS, we need courage to conquer. In this study of Daniel, you will be examining the Old Testament story of how God enabled not only Daniel but his three companions to conquer, when every circumstance seemed to be against them. It was through God's wisdom that these men of faith conquered in the midst of adverse circumstances. As you study God's timeless message you will discover that the principles have not changed!

It is only by the Lord's mighty power and wisdom that you can hope to conquer the daily circumstances that come your way. Daniel and his three companions made a conscious choice to obediently follow the commands of the Lord, their God. Thus the pagan King Nebuchadnezzar could say of them that they "yielded up their bodies so as not to serve or worship any god except their own God" (Dan. 3:28, *NASB*). They made their choice to obey God and so knew the Lord's victory in their circumstances. Even the pagan king gave honor to the one true God, as he watched these men given the courage to conquer.

If you want to find the power of God to have the courage to conquer in your life, you too must make the choice to obey God. The apostle Paul wrote about this choice in Romans 12:1,2: "With eyes wide open to the mercies of God, I beg you, my brothers, as an act of intelligent worship, to give him your bodies, as a living sacrifice, consecrated to him and acceptable to him. Don't let the world around you squeeze you into its own mould, but let God re-make you so that your whole attitude of mind is changed. Thus you will prove in practice that the will of God is good, acceptable to him and perfect" (*Phillips*).

As you study the book of Daniel, you will discover how a life surrendered to God can be mightily used to bring His love and hope to a world that somehow believes that love and hope are gone. You will discover how to find light in the midst of darkness that will not only give you courage to conquer but also enable you to help others find their courage in Christ Jesus. You will see the triumph God gave to

Daniel and his three friends, and thus you can be assured that you too can believe God to bring triumph in trials. Daniel's prayer and confidence in God will encourage your heart to trust God more than you ever have before. So let's join Daniel in finding courage to conquer through faith and trust in the Lord Jesus Christ day by day as we spend time in His Word!

HOW TO USE THIS BOOK

The Bible is a living book! It is relevant and powerful, but more than that, it is the active voice of our living God, and He wants to communicate with you daily through His Word. As you study the Bible, you will learn about God's person and character. You will begin to find His purpose for your life as He speaks to you through His written Word. His purpose is unchanging and His principles are unfailing guidelines for living. He will show us His truth and what our response should be to it.

Will you set aside a special time each day to interact with God in His Word? As you read, study, meditate and memorize His Word, the Holy Spirit will guide you, and His direction for your life will be made clear. More and more, His voice will be easily discerned in the din of life's pressures. When your heart is available and you see God's good intentions for you, you will then learn how to respond to the Lord's individual call to you day by day, moment by moment. As you train your ears to hear the voice of God, you will recognize His presence in the most unlikely circumstances and places. "The grass withers and the flowers fall, but the word of our God stands forever" (Isa. 40:8, *NIV*).

Will you choose to hear from God today? Open your Bible and turn to the study questions in Lesson 1. It is good to read the passage in several versions of the Bible, if you have them available. Each version may add new insights. Try not to use a commentary or any other reference book until you have allowed the Lord to personally speak to you from His word.

At the beginning of each set of questions, you will find suggestions for getting the most from your study of God's Word.

There are six sections of questions in each lesson. You will find it most beneficial to do one section daily. This will allow you time to meditate on God's Word and really hear what He has to say to you personally. When you have completed the questions, carefully read

9

the study notes, which follow, and look up the Scripture verses. This will give you added insight on the lesson you have just completed.

This study is designed to be used individually or in a group. If you're studying in a group, we urge you to actively share your answers and thoughts. In sharing we give encouragement to others and learn from one another.

May God bless you as you begin your journey into His Word. This may be the first time for you to take this trip, or it may be that you have journeyed this way many times before. No matter what trip it is for you, we pray you will find new joy and hope as you seek to live in the light of the living God!

DANIEL

= KINGS
(J) = JUDAH
(B) = BABYLON

600 BC
PROPHETS: JEREMIAH (J)

Daniel taken to
Babylon with
other captives.

650 BC
DANIEL (B)

KINGS:

JEHOIAKIM (J)

ZEDEKIAH (J)

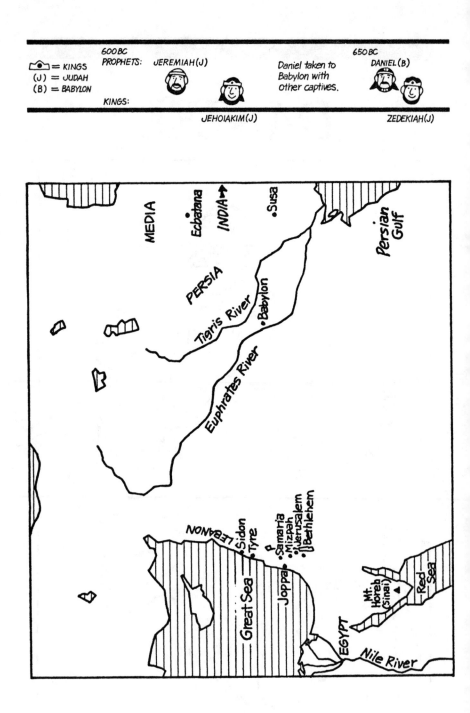

MEDIA

•Ecbatana

INDIA→

•Susa

Persian Gulf

PERSIA

Tigris River

•Babylon

Euphrates River

LEBANON

Sidon
•Tyre

•Samaria
•Mizpah
•Jerusalem
•Bethlehem

Great Sea

Joppa•

Mt. Horeb (Sinai)

Red Sea

EGYPT

Nile River

A MAN FOR ALL SEASONS

DANIEL 1

Before you begin your study this week:
1. Pray and ask God to speak to you through His Holy Spirit each day.
2. Use only your Bible for your answers.
3. Write your answers and the verses you have used.
4. Challenge questions are for those who have the time and wish to do them.
5. Personal questions are to be shared with your study group only if you wish to share.
6. As you study, look for a verse to memorize this week. Write it down, carry it with you, tack it to your bulletin board, tape it to the dashboard of your car. Make a real effort to learn the verse and its reference.

FIRST DAY: Read all of Daniel 1 concentrating on verses 1-4.

1. What country invaded Jerusalem? Who was the king of this country, and who was the king of Judah at this time?

2. According to Daniel 1:2, who was it that allowed Jehoiakim to be defeated?

13

3. **Challenge:** How does Isaiah 39:2-7 provide the background details as to why the Lord allowed this invasion to take place? Summarize briefly.

4. What was taken from the house of God in Jerusalem and put in a pagan house of god in Shinar (Babylon)? (see Dan. 1).

5. The king of Babylon wanted the best youths of Israel brought to Babylon to be trained in Babylonian culture. Who were the ones to be chosen by Ashpenaz and what characteristics were they to possess?

6 a. It is a real service to God to provide for the education of our youth. Do you believe that God would choose for us to give greater opportunities to those who are of a higher I.Q. and more attractive? Or do you believe He wants us to give equal attention to others with less aptitude, skill and physical attractiveness? (see Matt. 7:12).

   b. (Personal) Have you ever asked the Lord to use you in your church as a Sunday School teacher, or in some weekday teaching activity in order to train young people in "the way they should go," which of course is to love and obey God? (see Prov. 22:4,6). Name some ways you could help our young people today.

SECOND DAY: Read Daniel 1:5-8.

1. With what did the king of Babylon plan to nourish these outstanding young men from Judah while they lived in the land of the Chaldeans, and for how long a time would they be fed this?

2. Among the fine young men taken from Israel to Babylon, what were the names of four of them that came from the tribe (the children of) Judah?

3. List their Jewish names and the new names the prince of the eunuchs of the king of Babylon gave them.

4 a. These names were all pagan names that suggests that King Nebuchadnezzar was seeking to destroy every connection of those young men with their people, land and faith in the one true God. They were to be totally brainwashed to accept the Chaldean people, culture and pagan gods—idols, fire, light, sun. In society today, do you believe there are people like the king, who would seek to brainwash our young people to accept culture and "social gods" by various methods? What methods are used today to brainwash people not only in our lands, but around the world?

b. What can Christians do to combat such forces within their society to assure that their children will not be molded into the pattern of the corrupt elements in their particular culture?

c. **Challenge:** What guidelines do you find in the following Scriptures that could help a young person in our culture?

Psalm 119:9

Proverbs 8:32-33

1 Timothy 4:12

2 Timothy 2:22

d. (Personal) Which of the verses in 4c was your favorite? Why?

5 a. What did Daniel decide to do in Daniel 1:8?

b. Since Daniel was to become a spokesman and leader for the Lord, does Proverbs 31:4,5 apply to him?

6. (Personal) Have you ever felt the necessity of self-denial so that you would not become a stumbling block to yourself or to someone else? (see Rom. 14:21; 15:1). What have you given up for the sake of the Lord Jesus Christ?

THIRD DAY: Read Daniel 1:9-14.

1. What was the prince of the eunuchs concerned about when Daniel asked that they would not have to eat the king's meat and drink his wine in Daniel 1:8? Give verse.

2. What was Daniel's proposal to Melzar, the steward set over them by the prince of the eunuchs, in Daniel 1:12,13?

3. What was Melzar's decision concerning this plan?

4. How does Psalm 106:46 express God's loving care during Daniel's captivity?

5 a. In the Gospel of John we are instructed by God to "labor" for meat that endureth to eternal life. What does John 6:27,33,35,37 say about the Lord Jesus Christ who is the Bread of Life? Summarize in your own words and insert your name into these Scriptures if you wish.

   b. (Personal) Have you ever deliberately and consciously invited the Lord Jesus Christ (the Bread of Life) to come into your life to be your Savior and Lord, or is your spiritual hunger still not satisfied? Read Revelation 3:20 and Acts 4:10-12 to help you think about whether you want to say yes or no to the Lord Jesus.

6. **Challenge:** In heaven there will be given spiritual food that totally satisfies all who have received the Lord Jesus Christ as their Savior and Lord. He is called the Lamb of God in Revelation 22:1-3. How do these verses encourage you as a Christian?

FOURTH DAY: Read Daniel 1:15-17.

1. At the end of 10 days on their diet of vegetables and water, how did Daniel and his 3 Israelite friends look?

2. **Challenge:** As these young Israelites trusted God, we can trust Him today. Put your name in the following verses:

Psalm 33:20,21

Psalm 34:4,5

Philippians 2:13-15

2 Corinthians 3:18

3. (Personal) Which of the references in question 2 was your favorite? Why?

4. What did Melzar decide to do about the portion of food and wine that Daniel and his friends were supposed to be eating? (see Dan. 1:16).

5. What did God do for these four young men?

6. (Personal) In our day when half the world or more is starving and many in some countries are overeating, do you think you should make it a matter of prayer about how much you should eat?

FIFTH DAY: Read Daniel 1:18-21.

1. Look back at Daniel 1:5 and then read Daniel 1:18. How long was it before all of the Israelite youths saw the king after they were

given special food and their intellectual training in the culture, wisdom and language of Babylonia?

2. As the king observed and talked with them, who impressed him the most?

3. What do you discover about these four men in Daniel 1:20?

4. How long did Daniel remain in Babylonia according to Daniel 1:21?

5. What does Daniel 6:28 say about Daniel?

6. (Personal) Which verse from this lesson did you choose to memorize? Write it down by memory with the reference. Share with your discussion group if possible. Remember that there are many Christians in the world who have had their Bibles taken from them, and all they have left of God's Word is what they have memorized. How much of the Bible would you have hidden in your memory if your Bible were taken from you?

SIXTH DAY: Read all the Notes and look up the Scriptures.

1. What new thought did you find helpful in the Notes?

2. What personal application did you select to apply to your own life this week?

Study Notes

Daniel was the companion of kings. He was a leader of men. He was a pioneer in reform. Daniel, like Joseph, was God's candle shining in heathen darkness. He was chief statesman in the first empire of the world, chief advisor of a great monarch, and a great protector of his own people.

God gave Daniel favor and love in the sight of the court official, Ashpenaz. The feelings of Darius toward Daniel are revealed when he finds that a trap has been set for him. He "was sore displeased with himself, and set his heart on Daniel to deliver him" (Dan. 6:14, *KJV*).

No doubt Cyrus was greatly influenced by this aged statesman, approximately 80 years old at this time. Daniel probably showed him the prophecy that Jeremiah had written concerning him 100 years before he was born. This made Cyrus issue a decree for the rebuilding of the Temple at Jerusalem (see 2 Chron. 36:22,23; Ezra 1; Isa. 44:28; 45:1).

These particular chapters in the book of Daniel contain many heartwarming passages for the personal Christian life:

1. The surrendered life—(see Dan. 1:1-21).
2. Light amidst darkness—(see Dan. 2:20-22).
3. Triumph through trial—(see Dan. 3:17-25).
4. The reward of service—(see Dan. 5:17).
5. Prayer and confidence in God—(see Dan. 6:10-24).

One of Many Captives

These first six chapters are historical, yet easy to understand. Daniel lived at the close of the history of the divided kingdom of Israel. The Israelites were punished for sin at this time by God's allowing them to be taken into captivity into a strange land. Daniel was among those taken to Babylonia.

In 931 B.C. the division of Israel's monarchy occurred when it became a southern kingdom of Judah with Rehoboam as king, and a northern kingdom of Israel with Jeroboam as king. The northern kingdom existed for 209 years (931-722 B.C.) and then fell to the Assyrians. This northern kingdom had 19 kings and they were all described as wicked in the sight of God. The southern kingdom existed for 345 years (931-586 B.C.) and then fell to the Babylonians. Strangely enough it also had 19 kings, but the average length of their reign was longer than the northern kings. Eight of these 19 kings were considered good by God. Yet sin was still present in the south ern kingdom, which resulted in the captivity of Daniel's day. The captives were taken from Jerusalem to Babylon at three different times. Daniel's time of captivity was 605 B.C. when Nebuchadnezzar brought Jehoiakim to his knees and carried out hostages, among them Daniel and his three associates (see Dan. 1:1-6). Later in 597 B.C., on another expedition to Palestine after certain rebellious acts of the Judean kings, Jehoiakim and Jehoiachin, Nebuchadnezzar again made Jerusalem submit. This time he carried off 10,000 captives, most of them craftsmen. Among them was King Jehoiachin and the young prophet Ezekiel (see Ezek. 1:1-3; 2 Chron. 36:10; 2 Kings 24:8-20). By this time, Daniel had already been in Babylon as a captive eight years. Finally in 586 B.C., after a long siege, Nebuchadnezzar destroyed Jerusalem and the Temple of Solomon (see 2 Kings 25). At this time Daniel had been a captive for 19 years in Babylon.

Since little is known of Daniel's prior life to the time of his captivity, we must speculate on what his background was from what we read of him. One would assume that he must have been of either royal or noble descent to qualify for selection as one to be educated in the Babylonian court (see Dan. 1:3). We can definitely assume that his parents must have been devout people to account for Daniel's remarkable dedication to God. This dedication is seen in the five episodes in Daniel's life as a captive. Daniel always resolved to live righteously before God.

He Remained True to His God

The prophet Ezekiel, a contemporary of Daniel, having been taken captive in the second aspect of the captivity of Jerusalem in 597 B.C., discovered when he arrived in Babylon that although Daniel had risen to a height of influence, he maintained his true faith in God. He was so impressed by Daniel that he named him, along with Noah and Job, a great man of righteousness (see Ezek. 14:14,20).

As Ezekiel recognized, Daniel was used to maintain the honor of the true God in pagan Babylon. People of that day evaluated foreign gods by the prosperity of the people who worshipped them, and the size and success of their army! This meant that when Judah was taken captive by Babylon, Judah's God did not measure up well according to Babylonian standards. Their own gods appeared to be stronger. This was not pleasing to God, and He used Daniel to change the situation! Long before God used Joseph and later Moses in Egypt to bring honor to His name before the Pharaohs of their day.

Daniel, according to the history of Israel, worked for the welfare of his own people while they were in captivity. These captives in a foreign land were not treated as cruelly as we might expect. In fact there is evidence in historical writings that they lived in good farming areas and had their own homes. They enjoyed freedom of movement and continued their own religious institutions of elders, priests and prophets. They had adequate employment and even carried on correspondence with the people in Israel. God probably used Daniel to influence the kings as he worked from his high position in the government, one similar to a prime minister or chief statesman today.

Why was Daniel taken in the earliest captivity to Babylon? Undoubtedly it was God's plan to allow him to achieve such a high position before the other Judeans arrived; Daniel also may have had much to do with the return of the captives to Judah in due time. He was still alive at this time and held the highest position of his career, serving under King Darius (see Dan. 6:2,3). It is remarkable that he should have held such a prominent place of influence in the government, considering he was more than 80 years old! It was unmistakably God's hand that brought this about. Daniel undoubtedly had a great influence on King Cyrus who issued the decree permitting the Jews to return to their land.

The book of Daniel divides into two sections of six chapters each. The first section is historical and gives us many passages we can apply to our everyday lives as Christians. The second section is prophetical, and presents four important visions God gave to Daniel. We will be studying the historical division in this course and therefore will only cover the first six chapters of Daniel. We urge you to read the last half of the book of Daniel with its prophetic message and let God speak to your heart personally through your individual study.

History Is Foretold

Daniel's first vision occurred in Belshazzar's first year (553 B.C.; Dan. 7:1). Daniel was about 67 years old at this time. His second vision found in chapter 8 was given in Belshazzar's third year (551 B.C.). The third vision (chapter 9—538 B.C.) was given 13 years later in King Darius's first year. The fourth vision (chapters 10-12) came in Cyrus's third year (536 B.C., Daniel 10:1). Cyrus was the chief ruler with Darius serving under him and both began their reigns the same year. Because of these visions the book of Daniel has been called the book of revelation of the Old Testament. Because they foretell history involving the empires during and following Daniel's own day, all four visions concern some of the last day events, before Christ returns for the second time. Since there is such a different view of prophecy among different denominations, we urge you to read carefully the last six chapters of Daniel and let God guide and bless you through this reading.

22

One interesting fact about the book of Daniel is that it is one of the three books in the Old Testament that has an extensive section written in Aramaic. There are two other Old Testament books that have shorter Aramaic sections: Ezra 4:8—6:18, 7:12-26 and Jeremiah 10:11. The principle language of the Old Testament is Hebrew. The reason for the use of Aramaic seems to be because of the terms and subject matter of the section where it is found in Daniel. The material deals with matters concerning the Gentile world and apparently God communicated through Aramaic, the language of the Gentile world of that day. The Aramaic is used from Daniel 2:4 to Daniel 7:28. Some people refer to the Aramaic section as the "Gentile section" of Daniel and to the Hebrew language section as the "Jewish section" of the book of Daniel.

The Jewish people as a result of their exile not only had religious changes but cultural changes in their lives. There was a rise in synagogue worship rather than Temple worship, and also the adoption of a second language—Aramaic. Obviously the Jews picked up the Aramaic, which was the language of commerce and very similar to Hebrew (see 2 Kings 18:26). Therefore, many of the Jews were bilingual.

As in several other books of prophecy (see Jer. and Hos.) the author is also the chief actor in the events recorded. Jesus referred to the prophecies of this book as "spoken of by Daniel the prophet" (see Matt. 24:15; Mark 13:14). Our Lord's testimony is not simply that the book was named after Daniel, but that its prophecies were spoken by him.

This book itself clearly presents Daniel as the author of at least the last half of the book. Modern critical scholarship denies the authorship of the book to its main character, Daniel, primarily because the book presents remarkably detailed history until the time of Antiochus Epiphanes (Syrian ruler 175-164 B.C.). Liberal thinkers believe that such information could only have been written after the events had occurred. However, conservative Bible students who accept the fact of supernatural predictive prophecy given by God do not have this problem. It is this author's opinion that Daniel wrote the entire book given the title of Daniel. That Daniel must have written the first half, too, follows from the unity of the book. The two halves of the book are interdependent as can be seen from the comparison of Daniel's interpretation of Nebuchadnezzar's dream of chapter 2 and the revelations given directly through him in the visions of chapters 7 through 12. Also the terminology used in Daniel 2:28 and 4:2,7,10 are similar to that of Daniel 7:1,2 and 15. Finally, all chapters combine in the purpose of showing the supreme God of heaven who rules over all nations and is above all their "man-made gods."

A Life Without Blame

Daniel's whole life from the time of his captivity was spent in the great and glamorous city of Babylon, the ancient Hollywood! We study this book and see that there he lived a life without blame, and was well-favored. Ezekiel refers to him as a model of righteousness (see Ezek. 14:14-20; 28:3). Although Daniel was a captive, he rose to be prime minister of Babylon. The wonderful thing is that he always remained true to Jehovah God. Furthermore, no position, no matter how difficult, found him without trust in God. God is able, in all temptations, to keep us from falling (see Jude 24), unless we have deliberately placed ourselves at the fire of the enemy. This book of Daniel reveals the power of God and His universal sovereignty.

As we study Daniel, we will see God as:

1. God the Keeper (Daniel 1). God's power in keeping Daniel and his companions is shown. They were given understanding and wisdom above all the wise men of Babylon.

2. God the Revealer of Secrets (Daniel 2). God's power is shown in revealing the dream of Nebuchadnezzar to Daniel. None of the wise men of Babylon could do this.

3. God the Deliverer (Daniel 3). God's power is evident in delivering Daniel's three companions from the fiery furnace. These young men stood up alone against a nation, with the calm assurance that God would deliver them. Yet adding, "But if not, be it known unto thee, O king, that we will not serve thy gods, nor worship the golden image" (Dan. 3:18, *KJV*). This event occurred after they had been in Babylon about 20 years and God was demonstrating, in this most dramatic way, His power over all of the gods of this country.

4. God the Potentate (Daniel 4). God's power is shown in dealing with a mighty heathen monarch, Nebuchadnezzar. God struck the proud king while he was strolling on the roof of his magnificent palace, boasting of his power. He was driven from his kingdom to dwell among beasts, a victim of a strange form of insanity.

5. God the Judge (Daniel 5). God's power is shown in the judgment revealed to Belshazzar, son of Nabonidus, by the handwriting on the wall. That night the king was slain by the Persian army and his city was taken.

6. God the All Powerful (Daniel 6). God's power is revealed in the deliverance of Daniel from the lion's den. Remember that Daniel was an old man. When he was a young man of about 20, he was honored by the highest office in the whole empire. Now at 90 he was thrown into the den of lions. It seems that even the lions honored him because he honored God.

We Need to Be Reminded of God's Power

Today, perhaps more than in any other age, we need to be reminded of the power of God and His sovereignty. God's power is greater than world power. God is our keeper and deliverer. Today many feel imprisoned in a fiery furnace or in a lion's den. As we see that God gave Daniel and his companions great victory, we will realize that God can do the same thing for us today!

Daniel chapter 1 gives us a definite account of the beginning of the prophet's life and education. We learn more about Daniel in the Bible than any other prophet. The books of Isaiah, Jeremiah and Ezekiel begin immediately with divine visions. Daniel begins with the study of human learning, and afterwards is honored with divine visions.

> *Just because someone else has a different experience in serving the Lord . . . you should not feel that God cannot use you! Variety originated with God!*

It is wonderful to know the variety of methods that God takes in training up men and women for service to Him. Just because someone else has a different experience in serving the Lord from you, or a different educational background, a different cultural background, etc., you should not feel that God cannot use you! Variety originated with God! In fact we can see it as we look around us. There is not one human being in this world who has an exact duplicate, nor has there ever been someone exactly like you. Even identical twins have some differences. Indeed, God enjoys variety!

Daniel 1 begins with a description of the historical setting in which the captivity of Daniel and his friends took place. Jehoiakim, king of Judah had succeeded his brother on the throne. Nebuchadnezzar was not yet the king of Babylon but would become such before the summer was over. His father, Nabopolassar, had been struggling with the Egyptians for control of the Middle East for several years prior to this time, but in this particular year he was taken ill and had to remain at home. His army was entrusted to Nebuchadnezzar and the young crown prince made good by soundly defeating the Egyptians. When his father died before the summer ended, Nebuchadnezzar was made king.

The occasion when Nebuchadnezzar lay siege to Jerusalem and took Daniel and other captives was sometime between the battle of

Carchemish and the event of the coronation period. Nebuchadnezzar must have followed the retreating remnants of the Egyptian army for at least part of the way to Jerusalem and then gone on to the city. Jerusalem was the first city to be subjugated in his overall campaign to take all of the leading cities of the area for his domination.

Because he conquered the city, he demanded valuable plunder including sacred objects from the Temple and also captives among whom were choice young men like Daniel, Hananiah, Mishael and Azariah.

Only part of the precious vessels from the Temple were taken to Babylon at this time. The remainder were removed when Jehoiakim surrendered (see 2 Kings 24:13).

The removal of these vessels from the Temple to Babylon had been prophesied in Isaiah 39:3-7. Hezekiah, the king at this time, had allowed the Babylonians to visit him and had shown off all of his treasures in his own house and in his land. Isaiah told Hezekiah that the Lord would allow Babylon to one day carry off all these things and his sons (descendants) would become eunuchs in the palace of the king of Babylon. We see in Daniel 1:3-4 that this prophecy was fulfilled. "Then the king commanded Ashpenaz, his chief eunuch, to bring some of the people of Israel, both of the royal family and of the nobility, youths without blemish, handsome and skillful in all wisdom, endowed with knowledge, understanding learning, and competent to serve in the king's palace, and to teach them the letters and language of the Chaldeans" (RSV).

God's Kingdom Is Everlasting

In the first year Daniel was carried to Babylon, and continued there the whole 70 years (see Dan. 1:21). During this time all nations began to serve Nebuchadnezzar and his sons and his son's sons (see Jer. 25:11-13). Jeremiah saw within the compass of his own time the rise, reign and ruin of that monarchy; so that it was the affair of a single age. Such short lived things are the kingdoms of the earth! But the kingdom of heaven is everlasting.

Yes, things did not look good for Judah at this point. The best of their youth and the vessels from the house of God had been taken to Babylon. They were conquered and Jehoiakim was left in charge of Jerusalem. Yet God's kingdom did go on. Truly He does control the rulers of this earth. So often Christians feel discouraged with conditions in the world. They need to remember what Romans 13:1 says, "Let every soul be subject unto the higher powers. For there is no power but of God: the powers that be are ordained of God" (KJV). Are you praying for the governing authorities of your city, state and country? Remember that they have been instituted by God and that you are responsible to them, and most responsible as a Christian to pray for them.

The people of Judah could have become very discouraged with their authorities! Jehoiakim died and his son, Jehoiachin, came to the throne. He rebelled against Nebuchadnezzar who in 598 B.C. besieged Jerusalem again. Once more Jerusalem was not destroyed, but the king and his mother and all the vessels of the Temple were taken away to Babylon with an even larger group of captives. Over 10,000 craftsmen made this journey. Evidently among this latter group was Ezekiel (see 2 Kings 24:6-16). Then Zedekiah, the uncle of Jehoiachin, was made king and also later rebelled against Nebuchadnezzar. This time Nebuchadnezzar destroyed the Temple and burned Jerusalem. The sons of Zedekiah were slain in his presence, and then Zedekiah's eyes were put out. He, with the final deportation, went into captivity in the year 588 or 587 B.C. This fulfilled the prophecy recorded in Jeremiah 25:8-13.

Nebuchadnezzar had several reasons for wanting to take the youths from the royal family and the nobility back to Babylon. They would be promising, attractive and intelligent, therefore, they would be trophies to make a show of for the evidence and magnifying of his success in Judah. Also as hostages their parents in Judah would conduct themselves well in order that their young people might receive better treatment in Babylon. Nebuchadnezzar also intended that these young men serve him well. This is why he wanted them to be skillful in all wisdom, endowed with knowledge, understanding, learning, and competent to serve in the king's palace (see Dan. 1:4). They would need to learn the language of the Chaldeans and be able to adapt to the different culture.

It is interesting that the king of Babylon gave directions that they must not choose any deformed or ordinary young men, but that they must be skillful in all wisdom and knowledge, understanding science, quick and sharp, as well as good-looking. He chose the young because they were pliable and teachable and they would soon forget their own people and incorporate with the Chaldeans. He did not realize that those who truly loved God would not conform to this pattern!

This is a challenge to us to provide for the education of all of our youth. Have you ever asked the Lord to use you in your church as a Sunday School teacher, or in some weekday teaching activity in order to train young people in the way they should go?

Only the Name Is Different Daniel 1:5-8

Daniel and his friends were the children of Judah, the royal tribe and probably of the house of David, which had grown to be a large family through the generations.

The prince of the eunuchs in Babylonia changed the name of Daniel and his friends partly to show his authority over them and their subjection to him, and partly in token of their being naturalized and made Chaldeans. Their Hebrew names had something of God in them. Daniel's name meant "God is my judge;" Hananiah's name meant "the grace of the Lord;" Mishael's name meant "He that is the strong God;" Azariah's name meant "the Lord is a help."

To make them forget the God of their fathers, they were given names that reflected the Chaldean idolatry. Daniel was called Belteshazzar, which signified "the keeper of the hidden treasure of Bel." Bel was the name of the heathen idol worshiped in Babylon. Hananiah's name was changed to Shadrach, which carried the meaning of "illuminated by the sun-god" or "inspiration of the sun." The Chaldeans worshiped the sun. Meshach was the name given to Mishael and it meant "of the goddess Shach, under which name Venus was worshiped." Azariah was given the Babylonian name, Abednego, which means "the servant of the shining fire," or "the servant of Nego." The Chaldeans also worshiped fire.

Thus these young men who had to be old enough to make the adjustment to a foreign land psychologically, yet young enough to learn easily and come to feel at home in a new cultural setting were given totally new names of Babylonian character. This certainly must have been an order of the government, for the young men themselves would not have chosen to have their former names taken from them. Think of how unpleasant the situation was for them already—they had been forcibly taken from their home, friends, and from a familiar culture to live among complete strangers making a difficult adjustment to a new culture and a hard language. The new names suggest that it was the full intention of Nebuchadnezzar to destroy every vestige of connection between these young men and their people, land and religion. Heathenism was to replace worship of Jehovah God. They were to be totally brainwashed and a radical break with their past was signified by the change of their names.

The same kind of pressure and persecution goes on in communist countries today. In Russia in the high schools the students are brainwashed. Atheism is a part of the curriculum. If a Christian parent says, "We won't send our children to school because they will teach them communism," the authorities will step in and say, "Now look at these illiterate, backward, religious fanatics. They don't even want their children to be educated." Because of this the authorities will take their children away from them and put them in foster communist homes. Hundreds and hundreds of families who have so tactfully and lovingly won over the sympathy and confidence of their children find that when their children come home from school they can undo all the work that the communist teachers have done. But parents have to be careful. If they have a rebellious teenager, he can go to the authorities and say: "Look, my parents are ramming religion down my throat and I don't like it." Then the authorities will step in and put the children in foster communist homes. Actually this is exactly the pattern that Nebuchadnezzar used. He moved the young people away from their parents into Babylon where he could train them in the way he liked.

Did you ever stop to think that this could happen within your own country? Are you training your young people in your home, in your church, in your community so that if this should happen they will have a faith in the Lord Jesus Christ to lean upon and will remain true to the Living God, just as Daniel and his three friends did?

Food Fit for Idols

The king of Babylon had planned to nourish these outstanding young men from Judah with the very same meat and wine with which he nourished himself. "Daniel purposed in his heart that he would not defile himself with the portion of the king's meat, nor with the wine which he drank" (Dan. 1:8, *KJV*). From the king's point of view, it was a splendid menu. The Babylonians would have considered it an honor, and most foreigners would have welcomed such a special diet. Nebuchadnezzar wanted to provide good food for his potential workers so that they would be assured of good health, but also wanted their allegiance to the Babylonian religion. His food was regularly consecrated to the gods by offering a portion to them first. This meant that anyone who ate this food gave allegiance to these gods.

This presented a problem to Daniel and his friends. If they ate the food, it would appear that they were giving allegiance to the Babylonian gods. Such action might nullify their personal devotion to their own true God. Also this food was considered unclean as it had been forbidden by God to eat (see Lev. 11:44-47). Certain meats were specifically forbidden and meats offered to heathen idols also. Perhaps these young men were Nazarites to whom wine was forbidden also. "He shall separate himself from wine and strong drink, and shall drink no vinegar of wine, or vinegar of strong drink, neither shall he drink any liquor of grapes, nor eat moist grapes, or dried" (Num. 6:3, *KJV*).

After the announcement of the menu had been given, the four recognized that they had a decision to make. They were to eat this menu for three years (see Dan. 1:5) in order to prepare themselves to serve the king well. Since God had brought Daniel into a loving friendship with the prince of the eunuchs, he dared to request of him a special favor. Daniel asked that he not be required to defile himself by eating the meat and drinking the wine. Daniel asked to have a substitute diet provided (see Dan. 1:8). Normally, God's people are to obey the laws under which they live. There is only one exception: when the earthly law directly contradicts God's law (see Acts 5:29). Of course they took the risk of severe punishment and derision from their peers from Judah who went along with the king and ate the diet he prescribed.

Are You Willing to Take a Risk?

We always take a risk when we make a different decision than most of society does. Decisions are difficult in proportion to the attractions that exist for making the wrong decision! In so many situations, to decide one way is to do the will of God while to decide the other is to disobey Him. The way a person chooses each time is crucial to his Christian walk. The kind of decisions a person makes shows what kind of Christian he is. It also predicts what kind of Christian he will be tomorrow! People shape the degree of spiritual maturity they will show in the future by how they decide today (see Rom. 12:2).

The kind of decisions a person makes shows what kind of Christian he is. It also predicts what kind of Christian he will be tomorrow!

When Daniel and his three friends discovered that even their diet was to be a Babylonian diet, they must have spent long hours talking over how they would respond to this requirement. Their menu had already been prepared by God and they intended to place their orders from it. "Blessed are the undefiled in the way, who walk in the law of the Lord. Blessed are they that keep his testimonies, and that seek him with the whole heart. They also do no iniquity: they walk in his ways" (Ps. 119:1-3, *KJV*).

These young men knew that long ago Jehovah God had prescribed the diet for his people. They also had been taught that certain meats that had been offered by the heathen to idols were repulsive to the godly Israelite (see Lev. 11:44-47). The flesh from the king's table was doubtlessly slain according to pagan ritual and offered to a pagan god. The Jewish people were forbidden to eat this flesh (see Exod. 34:15).

30

A similar situation prevailed in regard to the wine, though some form of wine seemed to be used in this Jewish diet (see Ps. 104:15; Isa. 55:1; Neh. 5:18). However, there were many instructions against excessive use of wine (see Lev. 10:1-9; Prov. 20:1; 23:20,30,31; 31:4,5).

Wine is the only alcoholic beverage mentioned in the Scriptures, but today along with wine there are many other alcoholic beverages which have caused a great social problem all around the world. Official records show that of every 10 people who drink an alcoholic beverage, 4 will become problem drinkers, and 2 of those 4 will become hardcore alcoholics who give their whole life over to this uncontrollable compulsion.

It is interesting to note that there were certain religious orders who were forbidden to use wine (see Num. 6:1-20; Judg. 13:1-7; Jer. 35:1-14). Today, we have the organization known as Alcoholics Anonymous which forbids the use of any alcoholic beverage. These people continue to call themselves alcoholics for they realize that they can never take one drink for it is the beginning of the end as they cannot stop with one drink but must go on to further excesses. The Old Testament people had similar groups.

What is the Christian's responsibility as he faces such major problems in our society? The Christian should always keep his heart open and ready to tenderly speak and help those who have been taken captive by this habit. Each person is just as precious as the next. The Lord Jesus Christ loves one just as much as the other. He died for all of us. Perhaps if each of us considered carefully the verse in 1 Corinthians 8:9 we might be able to help the many around us who are fighting the battle of alcoholism. "But take heed lest by any means this liberty of yours becomes a stumbling block to them that are weak" (KJV).

Health Foods Then and Now Daniel 1:9-21

Melzar, the prince of the eunuchs, gave the four youths permission to have a 10-day trial of eating pulse (vegetables) and water. Then he would look at them and see how they had fared and decide whether to let them continue this diet. After the 10- day trial period, "Daniel and his three friends looked healthier and better nourished than the youths who had been eating the food supplied by the king! So after that the steward fed them only vegetables and water, without the rich foods and wines!" (Dan. 1:15, TLB).

Daniel's suggestion of the trial period displayed great faith. Not only would the four young men have to look no worse than the others at the end of the test period, but they would have to actually look better if this Babylonian officer was to be convinced. A period of 10 days was a short time for God to effect much of an improvement, but Daniel believed God would bring it about. It took faith on Daniel's part to believe that God would do this and God met him in that faith.

Since God had proved His faithfulness and the four were even in better physical condition than the others who were eating from the king's food, Melzar fed them pulse for the next three years. As a result, God favored these four youths with "knowledge and skill in all learning and wisdom" (v. 17, *KJV*). The word translated "learning" is again the word for "book." Doubtlessly these young men had mastered Babylonian literature. God gave them their knowledge, skill and wisdom, but it should be remembered that God regularly uses means to accomplish His purpose! The means in this instance must have been long hours of study. God has a plan for your life, but He wants you to do all you can by His help to bring it about.

God Gives Special Gifts

In addition to all these things, Daniel was given understanding in visions and dreams (see Dan. 1:20). This was a special ability given by God apart from any possible human study or effort. Daniel could never have learned to do this by himself. The Babylonians believed that you could learn to interpret dreams. Methods of divination had been devised, and serious attention was given to these methods by Babylonia's specialists. These methods had to be rejected by Daniel and the other three for they were forbidden by God. They are still forbidden today. God's Word does not change. One reason for mentioning Daniel's special gift may be to show that the four men did reject the Babylonian methods and that was why God gave Daniel special insight for interpreting dreams and visions. Another reason is to prepare the reader for Daniel's activities in giving such interpretations more than once in the following chapters of the book. However, for the ordinary Christian the Scriptures are very specific on God's rules concerning divination and sorcery. It is strictly forbidden (see Lev. 19:26-28,31; 20:6; Deut. 18:9-14). God denounced it in Isaiah 8:19; and Malachi 3:5. In Acts 19:17-20 we read, "And the name of the Lord Jesus was greatly honored. Many of the believers who had been practicing black magic confessed their deeds and brought their incantation books and charms and burned them at a public bonfire. (Someone estimated the value of the books at $10,000). This indicates how deeply the whole area was stirred by God's message" (*TLB*).

It was decided that Daniel and his three friends could continue their diet for three full years (see Dan. 1:5,18). Apparently an examination was given to all the young men on the completion of their three-year course of study and it was especially exciting for Daniel and his three friends as they stood before the king. In all matters of wisdom and understanding that the king inquired of them, he found them to be 10 times better than all the magicians and astrologers that were in all his realm! (see Dan. 1:19,20). In other words they were the "top four" at the graduation! The phrase "therefore stood they before the king" (Dan. 1:19, *KJV*) means that they were given positions of service above all of the other young men who were also given positions.

In Daniel 1:21 we read that Daniel continued in service in a high position even unto the first year of King Cyrus. Thus we realize that he continued to serve all the years of the Babylonian empire until the reign of Cyrus who brought this empire to an end. Daniel did not speak of himself continuing into the reign of Cyrus a few years as he did (see Dan. 10:1). This may indicate that he wrote at least this part of the book in the first year of Cyrus. He could not have known at that point, of course, just how much longer God would permit him to live. He had survived and outlived all of the kings from Nebuchadnezzar to Cyrus and now was an old man, possibly in his 90s. Evidently Daniel held the office of a wise man until his death. Why? Because he loved, trusted, and obeyed Jehovah God.

A GLIMPSE OF THINGS TO COME

DANIEL 2

Before you begin your study this week:
1. Pray and ask God to speak to you through His Holy Spirit each day.
2. Use only your Bible for your answers.
3. Write your answers and the verses you have used.
4. Challenge questions are for those who have the time and wish to do them.
5. Personal questions are to be shared with your study group only if you wish to share.
6. As you study, look for a verse to memorize this week. Write it down, carry it with you, tack it to your bulletin board, tape it to the dashboard of your car. Make a real effort to learn the verse and its reference.

FIRST DAY: Read all of Daniel 2 concentrating on verses 1-9.

1. What disturbing event happened to Nebuchadnezzar?

2. What unusual demands did Nebuchadnezzar make of his wise men and how did he threaten to punish them or reward them according to their words of interpretation? Give verses.

3. Notice in Daniel 2:2 that this pagan king called upon astrologers and sorcerers to interpret his dream. Astrology and sorcery is a rising tide in society today. What does God say about such things in the Bible? Read the following verses and summarize them briefly.

Leviticus 19:31

Deuteronomy 18:10-13

Galatians 5:19,20 (Note: These practices belong to the works of the flesh and are not the fruit of the Holy Spirit as found in Gal. 5:22-25.)

4 a. Do you believe that there are many people today like Nebuchadnezzar who depend upon magicians, astrologers and sorcerers (those who practice witchcraft and encourage the work of demons)? How do individuals depend upon such people today? Does this please God?

   b. (Personal) Have you any connection with any of these forms of pagan practices today? What do you believe you should do about this after reading what God says concerning these things in the Bible? Read 1 John 1:8-9; 5:3-5 to help you make your decision concerning this matter.

5. What can parents and youth leaders do to inform the younger generation about the dangers of the practices we read about in question 3 and 4?

6 a. What did Nebuchadnezzar claim about the dream he had in Daniel 2:5?

b. Challenge: Do you believe he had forgotten his dream, and if so why was he so troubled and wanted to know what it meant?

SECOND DAY: Read Daniel 2:10-13.

1. Who did the Chaldeans (the priestly class of the Babylonian religion according to the translation from the Aramaic language) say were the only ones who could tell Nebuchadnezzar his dream?

2. These priests did what Romans 1:22-23 describes. What was this?

3. **Challenge:** These Chaldean priests worshiped Venus, heathen idols, the sun and fire. Yet God had provided opportunities through the world He created for them to recognize Him as the one true God. What do these verses say about this?

Acts 14:16-17

Romans 1:18-20

4. (Personal) Do you believe there are many people today who also

ignore the evidence God gives of His power and His love for mankind? What are you doing to help them find Jesus Christ as their Savior and Lord?

5. Have you memorized John 3:16-18? Write it down here and try to commit it to memory. It is a good portion of Scripture to always have on hand.

6. What did Nebuchadnezzar demand in Daniel 2:13 because his dream had not been interpreted?

THIRD DAY: Read Daniel 2:14-23.

1. What did Daniel ask Arioch, the king's captain of the guard? Then with great courage from God what did he ask of King Nebuchadnezzar in Daniel 2:16?

2 a. In Daniel 2:17-18 where did Daniel go and what happened there? Do you believe this was the first "youth" prayer meeting in the Bible? Was the prayer recorded for us?

b. (Personal) Do you have a prayer partner or a prayer group to which you can go when needs arise in your life? Perhaps someone in your neighborhood or in your Bible Study group is also looking for prayer partners. You can even pray by telephone if distances separate you.

3. **Challenge:** There is much about prayer in the Bible. What do you learn about prayer from the following verses?

Psalm 116:2

John 9:31

Romans 10:13

4. Read Daniel 2:19. How was the youth's prayer to God answered?

5. Daniel then prayed a prayer of praise to God, and we would imagine his three friends joined in praising prayer with him! Give the highlights of this recorded prayer from Daniel 2:20-23 with verses.

6. (Personal) So often we ask God for many things, but often we forget to praise Him for who He is, for His blessings, His help, His answers to our prayers. Why not make a list of praise items in this space and then bow your head and in Jesus' name praise God?

FOURTH DAY: Read Daniel 2:24-35.

1. What did Daniel tell Arioch? Did Daniel get to see the king?

2. To whom did Daniel give credit for the interpretation of his dream? Whom did he say could not give the secret of the king's dream? Give verses please.

3 a. Did Daniel take any credit for the interpretation of the dream?

   b. Why did God make the dream known to Daniel?

4. **Challenge:** Read Daniel 2:31-35 and briefly describe the dream God gave Daniel. Give verses please.

5. In the word "stone" in Daniel 2:35 we see the kingdom of Christ whose kingdom shall never be destroyed. Briefly state what the Bible says about the "Stone." (Note: *Builders* refers to the Jewish people, the Israelites.)

   Psalm 118:22

   Isaiah 28:16

6. Read 1 Peter 2:3-8 but write down only the verse that means the most to you concerning Jesus Christ, "the Stone," and the "Chief Corner Stone."

FIFTH DAY: Read Daniel 2:36-49.

1 a. How did Daniel point out the power of God in heaven to the king?

   b. (Personal) How often do you take advantage of opportunities to give glory to God and recognize His power, as Daniel did before the king? Should you pray for boldness and the leading of the Holy Spirit for yourself in this area (see 1 Thess. 1:5)?

2. **Challenge:** Describe what each part of the image seen in the dream symbolized. Use only your Bible for your answer. Give verses please.

3. Were there any important or encouraging facts to be found in Daniel 2:44?

4. What does Daniel say that the great God has shown to the king through this dream?

5. How did Nebuchadnezzar respond to Daniel's God in Daniel 2:47? Certainly we see that Daniel had maintained God's honor in a pagan palace through these statements of the king!

6 a. In what ways did the king honor Daniel? At the request of Daniel how did the king also honor Daniel's three prayer partners?

b. Which verse from this lesson did you choose to memorize?

SIXTH DAY: Read all the Notes and look up the Scriptures.

1. What new thought did you find helpful in the Notes?

2. What personal application did you select to apply to your own life this week?

Study Notes

Nebuchadnezzar's dream and its interpretation teaches us some very interesting things about the history of the world from that time until the end of this age. This period the Bible calls the times of the Gentiles, because God has put aside his own people, the Jews, for a time and has passed over the government of the world to the Gentiles. Daniel 2 has been called the "ABC of Prophecy." It stretches out before us the most complete picture in all the Scriptures of what is to come—the future.

What's in a Dream? Daniel 2:1-13

All of chapter 2 concerns Nebuchadnezzar's dream, which occurred during the second year of his reign. Thus there is some confusion about this "second year of the reign." Daniel and his friends had studied for three years in Nebuchadnezzar's kingdom and in Daniel 1:18 the king had examined them himself. They had been found to be the wisest of all of the trainees that had been brought to Babylon from Israel as captives. The most probable solution to this "second year" is that the author followed a custom that was certainly often adopted by Jewish writers and was generally used in Assyria and Babylonia. They postdated the reigning years of a king, counting his first year not the year of his ascension, but the first full year afterwards. Thus if Nebuchadnezzar gave orders for the education of the Jewish youths in his ascension year, the end of three years would be recorded as falling within the king's second year.

Nebuchadnezzar used his dream as a way of testing the authenticity of the Babylonian wise men. The king wanted his dream interpreted and so he called the magicians, astrologers, sorcerers and the Chaldean priests to tell him what his dream meant. Certainly he must have remembered the dream or it wouldn't have bothered him so much, yet he claimed that he had forgotten the contents of it and insisted the wise men not only interpret the dream but also tell him what the dream was (see Dan. 2:3-5).

Nebuchadnezzar gave a terrible threat along with his request. "If you won't tell me what [my dream] was and what it means, I'll have you torn limb from limb and your houses made into heaps of rubble!" (Dan. 2:5, *TLB*). This threat and extreme penalty helps us to understand that Nebuchadnezzar was suffering from a mental problem, which we will see in chapter 4. He was ruled by an uncontrollable temper. What about you? Do you allow Jesus Christ to replace your anger by the fruit of the Spirit as shown in Galatians 5:22-23? (see also Prov. 15:1,18).

In Daniel 2:7,10, and 11 the wise men responded to the king that they would gladly give an interpretation, but they could not tell the dream. They even rebuked the king in verse 10 by telling him that no other king had ever made such a demand. What they said was quite true, for it was normal for a king to accept the interpretation of the wise men without question. They nicely prepared the way for Daniel's entrance on the scene by saying in Daniel 2:11, "There is none other that can show it before the king, except the gods, whose dwelling is not with flesh" (KJV). Daniel was able to give the information that had been given to him by the true God of heaven.

We notice in Daniel 2:2 that this pagan king called upon his astrologers and sorcerers to interpret his dream. Astrology and sorcery is a rising tide in our society today. God has much to say about such things in the Bible. "I will even set my face against [anyone who consults mediums, and wizards instead of me, and I] and will cut him off from among his people. Sanctify yourselves therefore, and be ye holy: for I am the Lord your God" (Lev. 20:6,7, KJV). In Deuteronomy 18:10 God warns against practicing black magic, calling on evil spirits for aid, or being a fortune teller. He also warns against serpent charmers, mediums, wizards, or any who call for the spirits of the dead. He says, "Anyone doing these things is an object of horror and disgust to the Lord" (Deut. 18:12, TLB). In the New Testament all of these things are called the works of the flesh and God says that they encourage the works of demons (see Gal. 5:19,20). Today drugs are used in connection with all of these things mentioned in the Scriptures and therefore are a part of this culture that is an abomination to the Lord.

Your decision to receive Jesus Christ determines your destiny.

Anyone participating in any of these activities can say with the Psalmist, "The sorrows of death compassed me, and the pains of hell got hold upon me: I found trouble and sorrow" (Ps. 116:3, KJV). Astrology was originally a religion and each of the planets was a god to be feared and worshiped. The Babylonians worshiped Venus as a god. Though most modern astrologers do not think of their practice as that of a religion, the basic interpretations of astrology are still derived from the ancient Chaldean belief that the planets have a divine personality and determine man's destiny. Modern astrology is gilted paganism. There are people today who will not do anything without looking at their astrological chart.

Finding Life's True Meaning

The search for true meaning in life is satisfied only when you turn in faith to the Lord Jesus Christ. The astrologers say your destiny is in the stars. The Christian faith declares that your decision to receive Jesus Christ determines your destiny (see John 3:16-18). It may be somewhat comforting to believe that we are not responsible for what we are, that celestial powers have impelled or compelled us to act, but it is not biblical! Paul wrote that we must all stand before God and give an account of ourselves (see Rom. 14:12). In that day, God will not allow such lame excuses as, "My stars weren't right that day."

We have covered only one area of temptation to dabble in what the Bible forbids in our day. Many choose to read tarot cards, consult palm readers, become practicing witches, participate in demon worship, join satanic worship groups, particularly hoping to speak to their loved ones who have departed from this world, and through drugs escape into the spirit world. None of these things please God. They are strictly forbidden in the Bible.

We also have a responsibility as parents, youth leaders, or persons who have an influence on young people to inform them of the dangers of such practices. We need to teach them the Scriptures concerning these things, warn them of the results and cite examples of such practices in our own day. We must also be willing to take time to pray for our young people that they will not be tempted in these areas. Last but not least, we need to set an example for them by not practicing and participating in such activities even "just for fun."

Wise for His Years Daniel 2:14-23

Daniel had been only about 16 years old when he was brought as a captive into Babylon, so at the most he was probably 19 or 20 at this time. The visit of a squad of executioners would have been a terrifying experience for Daniel and his young friends, but it was a way of permitting Daniel an entrance before Nebuchadnezzar so that he might give him God's interpretation of the dream.

Daniel, puzzled by this hasty and unjust decree of the king, used tact in approaching Arioch, the captain of the king's guard. It would be interesting to know all that Arioch communicated to Daniel. Did he suggest that the king was "off his rocker"? It is not recorded! (see Dan. 2:14,15). Daniel gained an audience with the king and asked him if he could be given time to tell the dream (see Dan. 2:16). Daniel's appearance before Nebuchadnezzar must have been a memorable experience for him.

We can imagine him dressing in his finest clothing for the occasion. Undoubtedly he was anxiously helped by his three friends. They probably all counseled him on how to behave before such a monarch! Visualize him being ushered in before the most powerful king in the world. The scene must have been resplendent with guards, attendants at hand, plush rugs and tapestries, and the king seated upon his throne. Just to stand there before him would be a nerve-wracking experience!

However, Daniel did not waver. He spoke the words God gave him and requested that he be given some time so that he might learn and bring back to the king the interpretation of the dream. This act took courage and faith on Daniel's part, for by this request he was agreeing to do what all the older wise men had failed to do! He promised the king that he would return with the information at the time the king would set.

You may wonder about dreams and interpretations in our day. But this dream was God's answer to Nebuchadnezzar's pagan heart. He held a high position as a world ruler and God wanted to get his attention. Until the Scriptures were completed, God spoke to men in dreams and visions as well as by other means of communication. Now that the Scriptures are completed, God speaks to men through His Word, the Bible. There are some jungle tribes who do not have the Bible translated in their language nor can they read. God still reveals Himself to them through dreams and other special signs. Missionaries have told how they have found people with a remnant of faith in the Lord because of special signs God has given them. It has made the way easier to reach them with the message of Jesus Christ. However, in our modern society God has given us the Bible and it is the norm by which He speaks to civilization.

As soon as Daniel had obtained permission to interpret the king's dream he rushed home and with his three friends he had the first teenagers' prayer meeting that was probably ever held (see Dan. 2:17,18). Hananiah, Mishael and Azariah joined Daniel in asking the mercies of God in heaven concerning this secret dream. "The God of heaven" is an expression peculiar to the books of the captivity (see Neh. 1:4). Since Jerusalem had been destroyed and the Temple burned, God no longer dwelt between the cherubims. Ezekiel saw the departure of the Shekinah glory to heaven (see Ezek. 9:3; 10:4,18; 11:23). God is now the God of heaven.

The phrase *desires mercies* reveals the basis of their prayer. God does not answer prayer because of the worth, effort, character or works of the one praying. All prayer rests upon His mercy. To pray in

Jesus' name means simply this: We come to God, not on our merit, but on His merit (see Rom. 5:14-16).

The Importance of Prayer

Prayer is an important part of the Christian life. Do you have a prayer partner to whom you can go in times of need, or a prayer group where you can ask others to pray with you? There are other Christians who need partners in prayer, too, and God will show them to you if you ask Him. You can even pray by telephone if distance separates you from your prayer partner.

The secret of the dream was revealed to Daniel in a night vision and Daniel blessed the God of heaven for this (see Dan. 2:19). The *Berkeley* version of the Bible suggests that God let Daniel dream the identical dream that Nebuchadnezzar had had. This could have been the way in which God communicated the dream to Daniel. Imagine how excited Daniel was as he quickly woke the other three from their sleep to tell them the answer to their prayers! He probably related the whole dream to them. Then the four young men had another youth prayer meeting, this time praising the Lord (see Dan. 2:20-23). Perhaps it is significant that the first prayer was not recorded. It was a prayer of request and God is more interested in praise than in request, though as many Scriptures make clear, He is very interested in our requests.

Christians tend to be much shorter in their praise than in their requests.

However, Christians tend to be much shorter in their praise than in their requests when they pray! Daniel was not short in his praise and this is an example for us. In fact the prayer he made that night was entirely made up of praise. Daniel praised God, speaking of His power and wisdom. He cited examples of this: God changes times and seasons through His control of history; He removes and establishes kings; He gives wisdom and knowledge where needed, as Daniel had just received it. In James 1:5 Christians are promised: "If you want to know what God wants you to do, ask him, and he will gladly tell you, for he is always ready to give a bountiful supply of wisdom to all who ask him; he will not resent it" (*TLB*). Daniel also stated that God revealed the information not known or knowable in any other way for He knows what is "in the darkness."

Daniel becomes very specific in Daniel 2:23: "I thank thee, and praise thee, O thou God of my fathers, who hast given me wisdom and might, and hast made known unto me now what we desired of thee: for thou hast now made known unto us the king's matter" (*KJV*). God alone had revealed the secret of the dream and its meaning to Daniel. Daniel gave praise to God in both a general and a specific manner. This is a fine example for Christians and, we are to do the same (see Luke 17:11-18).

All Glory and Power to God Daniel 2:24-45

Daniel went to Arioch whom the king had appointed to destroy all the wise men of Babylon if his dream could not be told and interpreted to him. He pleaded with Arioch not to destroy the wise men of Babylon but to take him to the king so that he could interpret the dream. Arioch rushed Daniel into the presence of the king with the good news that the dream would be divulged. Apparently he had not relished his assigned task of killing all of the wise men of Babylon! (see Dan. 2:24,25).

Obviously the king was skeptical that this young man would be able to do what all the other wise men were unable to do. He asked, "Art thou able to make known unto me the dream which I have seen, and the interpretation thereof?" (Dan. 2:26, *KJV*). Daniel answered immediately that, "There is a God in heaven that revealeth secrets, and maketh known to the king Nebuchadnezzar what shall be in the latter days" (Dan. 2:28, *KJV*). Daniel gave credit not to himself but to the God of heaven and pointed out that all the wise men, astrologers, magicians and soothsayers had been unable to show the king what the God of heaven was about to reveal through Daniel (see 1 Cor. 1:18-25). It was Daniel's great privilege to introduce the living and true God—"The God of heaven"—to the darkened mind of this pagan king. Have you ever allowed God to use you to introduce Jesus Christ to one who has "been in the dark" without Him as Savior?

Daniel pointed out in verse 29 that while the king had been lying on his bed, thoughts came to him of what would be hereafter; not meaning life after death but of the future in general. The king was probably thinking about his own kingdom and its future and the meaning of the dream did include Nebuchadnezzar's kingdom as well as other great empires to succeed him. Daniel proceeded to explain the image that the king had seen in his vision. The head was of gold; its breasts and arms were silver; the belly and thighs were brass; and its legs were iron, with feet and toes of iron and clay. Then a Stone cut out without hands smote the image and broke it to pieces; and the Stone became a great mountain and filled the whole earth. This Stone was none other than the Lord Jesus Christ! (see Isa. 28:16; Ps.

118:22; Matt. 21:42-44; 1 Peter 2:3-8). All of these details about the great image that Nebuchadnezzar had seen are found in Daniel 2:31-35 and the interpretation of what he saw is found in Daniel 2:36-45. First of all Daniel gave all of the glory for the interpretation of the dream to the God of heaven (see Dan. 2:37,38). He told the king that it was the God of heaven who had given him his kingdom, power, might and glory, and it was the God of heaven who had given him to rule over the sons of men, the beasts of the fields and the birds of the air. Daniel took no credit for the interpretation of the dream, but gave all of the glory and honor to God. Often Christian workers need to be reminded of this for truly it is God who empowers and guides by His Holy Spirit (see Zech. 4:6). We need to remember, like Daniel, to give the glory to God!

God Speaks of the End Times

God first revealed the Gentile powers through this dream. Four great empires were to succeed each other in the government of the world from Nebuchadnezzar to the end times. God said, "Thou art this head of gold" (Dan. 2:38, *KJV*). The breasts and arms of silver represented the Medo-Persian empire, which overthrew Babylon and became its successor. Its power began with Cyrus under whom the Jews returned to Jerusalem (see Ezra 1:1,2). The belly and thighs of bronze (brass) represented Greece, which overturned the Medo-Persians. It pictures the Grecian rule "over all the earth" under Alexander the Great. This interpretation is established by Daniel 8:20,21. This kingdom replaced that of the Medes and the Persians when Alexander, in a series of advances beginning in 334 B.C., overcame the Medes and Persians. The fourth kingdom of iron (see Dan. 2:40-43) is representative of the Roman Empire, which appears to prevail to this present day.

From then on we find an ever-dividing kingdom and a government ever-weakened in its power represented by toes of iron and clay that cannot hold together (see Dan. 2:41-43). More is said of this fourth Gentile government than of the others. Perhaps because it is the last. There will be a division into as many kingdoms as the toes. There is deterioration represented by the feet and toes being part iron and part clay that cannot hold together. This last government will be the weakest. It will not be completely unified, and will finally end in chaos.

In the "Stone" cut out without hands we see the kingdom of Christ, whose kingdom shall never be destroyed, bringing to an end all other kingdoms. Christ will come and set up a kingdom that will last forever (see Dan. 2:44,45). There is disagreement about interpretation rooted in the varying points of view in which readers approach this passage. Therefore, we will not go into the details of this interpretation but only emphasize that one day the prophecy will be fulfilled and the kingdom of Christ will be set up on earth.

Since the book of Daniel is prophetic, we are told of the coming of Christ to set up His kingdom (see Dan. 2:45). *Unger's Bible Dictionary* says, "Widespread attempts to 'bring in the kingdom' on the basis of Christ's first advent have been misplaced. According to the clear teaching of the Bible it will be realized only in connection with the second advent. The testimony of Scripture agrees completely with this fact. According to Matthew 13 the present gospel age represents the mystery form of the kingdom." Christ said that the Kingdom of God was within the Christian; it cannot be visibly seen (see John 3:3-8). In that wonderful day of His coming, He will then set up His kingdom, which every eye will be able to see.

Remember at the time Nebuchadnezzar dreamed his dream the Persian kingdom did not exist. It was merely a Babylonian province. It would have seemed impossible that a strong Grecian Empire would arise. Only wandering tribes inhabited the Hellenic states. The city of Rome was only a little town on the banks of the Tiber River. Yet God told Daniel what would come to pass!

Notice that the metals in the image deteriorate in value—gold, silver, brass and iron. This reveals the weakening in the power of each succeeding empire. Finally we will find a condition of iron mixed with brittle clay suggesting attempted unions between a democratic and an imperialistic form of government. Name the forms of government that exist today. Do these resemble the toes of clay, brittle and not holding together?

Many ask, "When will this stone fall?" We know not the day nor the hour but King Jesus is coming with power and great glory and with all His holy angels to establish His kingdom (see Phil. 2:9; 1 Tim. 6:15; 1 Pet. 3:22). "The kingdoms of this world are become the kingdoms of our Lord, and of his Christ; and he shall reign for ever and ever" (Rev. 11:15, *KJV*). One day this will all come about, but only God knows the hour and the day. Our chief concern should be our readiness for that day. Have we received the God of heaven's Son, the Lord Jesus Christ, as Savior and Lord?

Honored by the King Daniel 2:46-49

The last part of this chapter concerns the response of the king to these significant words of Daniel. He highly honored the young man and praised the God to whom Daniel had given all the credit. He actually bowed before Daniel and called for offerings and sweet incense to be given to him. Bowing before a mere captive was an incredible action of this emperor! What changes God can effect in a person's heart! Nebuchadnezzar had pointed out that it was the God of heaven who had given the information, so it is doubtful that Nebuchadnezzar was worshiping Daniel but only seeking to worship this God through Daniel. His words brought forth this truth, "Your God is a God of gods, and a Lord of kings" (Dan. 2:47, *KJV*). The king was actually admitting that Daniel's God was greater than the gods of Babylon.

Then Nebuchadnezzar gave Daniel many great gifts (see Dan. 2:48) and made Daniel ruler over the whole province of Babylon. The empire was divided into several provinces each with a governor. The most important province was Babylon, the capital. Also Daniel was made chief over all the governors and wise men of Babylon. The greatest honor of all was for such a young man to be put in charge of all the other wise men. Daniel would have frequent and significant contact with the mighty king and would have a strong influence on him. God had been truly faithful to Daniel as Daniel had been obedient to His will. It seemed just a few months before that neither he nor his friends would obtain any position at all because of the choice they made to eat the simple food rather than the rich foods and wines from the king's table.

God Honors Those Who Honor Him

It is heartening to see that Daniel did not forget his three friends who had been through the hardship with him, prayed with him and indeed must have been praying while Daniel stood before the king interpreting the dream. In Daniel 2:49 he asked on their behalf that they be appointed over the affairs of the province of Babylon. The king agreed to this. Since it says in verse 49 that Daniel "sat at the gate of the king," the king realized that he would need to have Daniel close to him; Daniel would be like a Supreme Court Justice along with his other positions. The gates corresponded to the court house in the square of a typical American city (see Gen. 19:1; Ruth 4:1; Esther 2:19).

God honors those who honor Him. What about you and me? Apart from Christ, nothing of eternal value can be done by us or through us. As we think of the work ahead, therefore, we need to realize our incompetence. We must realize that if anything is to be accomplished by us on earth, it will be done only because God does it for us, through us and first of all in us. We are acceptable to serve God when we know that we depend on His Spirit. We must realize that even though in ourselves we are incompetent, we must not quit, but look to Christ for encouragement, strength and purpose.

SERVANTS OF THE MOST HIGH GOD
DANIEL 3

Before you begin your study this week:
1. Pray and ask God to speak to you through His Holy Spirit each day.
2. Use only your Bible for your answers.
3. Write your answers and the verses you have used.
4. Challenge questions are for those who have the time and wish to do them.
5. Personal questions are to be shared with your study group only if you wish to share.
6. As you study, look for a verse to memorize this week. Write it down, carry it with you, tack it to your bulletin board, tape it to the dashboard of your car. Make a real effort to learn the verse and its reference.

FIRST DAY: Read Daniel 3 concentrating on verses 1-7.

1 a. Give the details that you find in Daniel 3:1 concerning the object Nebuchadnezzar made.

b. See if you can locate the area mentioned in Daniel 3:1 on a map. Where is this area in relation to Jerusalem and the Dead Sea?

2 a. Who did the king ask to come for the dedication of the image, and where did these people come from?

   b. Where did Nebuchadnezzar gather them together?

3 a. According to Daniel 3:4 what variety was represented in this group?

   b. Idolatry is a perversion of man's need for God. At what sound were all of these people asked to fall down and worship this new idol?

   c. What would happen to those who refused to worship this new god?

4. **Challenge:** Many Scriptures warn us about idols. What do the following say?

   Exodus 20:4,5

   Romans 1:22,23 (how do these verses describe men who make and worship idols?)

   1 John 5:21

5 a. What are the present-day "idols" that keep people from wor-

shiping the Lord Jesus Christ? Examples could be anything that becomes such an obsession in a person's life that it leaves no room for the worship of God. It might not be made of gold or silver; it might not be a graven image; it might simply be a hobby, intellectual pursuit, materialism, etc. Nothing like this is wrong and condemned by God unless it becomes an "idol" to the person pursuing it. Give examples of what you think people in our generation have made into "idols".

b. Reread Exodus 20:4,5. How do you believe parents can harm their own children, grandchildren and great-grandchildren by choosing to serve a present-day idol?

c. (Personal) Look very carefully at your own life. Do you find any idols that are placed higher and more important in your life than your worship of the Lord Jesus? What does Psalm 139:23,24 say concerning this? Should this be your prayer?

SECOND DAY: Read Daniel 3:8-13.

1. Who had been the "lookouts" for the king and whom did they accuse?

2. What did the Chaldeans accuse these Jews of doing? (see Dan. 3:12).

3. What was the king's response to this report, and what did he demand?

4. Surely these three young men must have trembled as they stood before this mighty monarch. Yet they chose to obey God above this great king. They would not be tempted to compromise

their faith. They would obey and be true to the God of heaven. What did Peter and the other apostles say in Acts 5:29 after they were told that they should not teach in the name of the Lord Jesus?

5. Put your name into these verses and personalize them for your life.

Proverbs 1:33

Matthew 6:24

THIRD DAY: Read Daniel 3:14-18.

1 a. What did Nebuchadnezzar personally ask these three young Jewish men?

b. Did he offer them a second chance to avoid the fiery furnace?

2. **Challenge:** In Daniel 3:15 music is mentioned. All music is not wrong! Music can be a wonderful aid to worshiping Jesus Christ the Lord. What do the following verses say about music?

1 Chronicles 16:8,9

Ephesians 5:19

Colossians 3:16

3. (Personal) Which of these verses gave you a challenge about singing to the glory of the Lord? You can sing in your home, your car, in your church choir, in the woods! Do you need to learn some hymns?

4. Were Shadrach, Meshach and Abed-nego afraid of the king and the fiery furnace? Find out by reading their reply to the king in Daniel 3:17,18.

5. (Personal) Today, many Christians around the world are threatened by their government to submit to its authority above God's authority. Do you believe that God could give the same courage to people today that He gave to these three young Jewish lads long ago? Do you believe He could give this same courage to you?

6 a. God promises to give us courage and His power in such situations. Put your name into the following verses.

1 Chronicles 28:20

Psalm 121:3

Philippians 4:19

b. (Personal) Which of these verses was most encouraging to you?

FOURTH DAY: Read Daniel 3:19-27.

1. What was the king's response when the three youths refused to bow to his idol?

2 a. What happened in Daniel 3:20,21?

  b. What happened to the men who threw the youths into the hot furnace?

3 a. What did the king see inside the fiery furnace that amazed him?

  b. What did the king call the three youths in Daniel 3:26 and what did he tell them to do?

4. What did all who watched them leave the furnace observe about these three young men?

5. These young men weren't striving to get out of the fire, but just walked up and down in the furnace, waiting to see what God would do. They seemed unconcerned and did not try to run out of the furnace! Are you going through some trial? God is with you in your "fiery furnace" if you have received Him as your Lord and Savior. What does 1 Peter 3:16,17 say concerning this?

6 a. These verses can be an encouragement to anyone who is in a "fiery furnace" of circumstances, or may be given by you to someone who needs encouragement in his trouble. God will help those who call out to Him. Put your own name into these verses.

Psalm 61:3

Isaiah 43:2

1 Peter 3:12,13

b. (Personal) Do you know someone with whom you should share one of these verses? Do it today, as the Holy Spirit leads you.

FIFTH DAY: Read Daniel 3:28-30.

1. Did King Nebuchadnezzar recognize who had saved the three youths from the fiery furnace?

2. What did the king say about how these three young men had yielded their bodies? (see Dan. 3:28).

3. What does Romans 12:1,2 say about the follower of the Lord Jesus Christ yielding his body?

4. (Personal) Reread Romans 12:1,2. What does this really mean to you in your life? Have you ever done this "yielding"? Are you conformed to this world in some way? What changes need to be made in your life? Who will provide the power to make these changes? (see Acts 1:8 and Zech. 4:6).

5 a. What decree did the king make in Daniel 3:29?

  b. What honor did he bestow on the three youths?

6. Which verse from this lesson did you choose to memorize? Write it down by memory with the reference. Share with your study group.

SIXTH DAY: Read all the Notes and look up the Scriptures.

1. What new thought did you find helpful in the Notes?

2. What personal application did you select to apply to your own life this week?

Study Notes

Daniel chapter 3 shows the rebellion of King Nebuchadnezzar against the God of heaven who had given him world dominion (see Dan. 2:37,38). It is apparent that Nebuchadnezzar planned to use this image as a unifying principle to weld together all the tribes, languages and peoples of his kingdom into a totalitarian government. He sent for all the princes, governors, captains, judges, treasurers, counsellors, sheriffs and rulers of his provinces for the dedication of this image. Many of these people had been conquered by him and brought into his kingdom. Now he would test their loyalty through worship of the image of gold.

Shadrach, Meshach and Abed-nego were in the province of Babylon at this time. Daniel is not mentioned at all. Perhaps Daniel was ill, or he may have been out of the country on business for the king, for you remember that one of his appointments was similar to what we would call a prime minister today (see Dan. 2:49). He may have been in one of the outlying provinces taking care of business that made it essential for him to stay until his task was finished. In this chapter Daniel's three young friends are the central figures. God directed Daniel to include this story to let us know that they also had true faith in God.

The date when this episode happened is not given. We know it would have been at least after the three years of training because the three young men had been appointed officers in the land in Daniel 2. Nebuchadnezzar commanded all of his officials to bow before a great statue, which quite clearly represented the gods of Babylon. The king had a fiery furnace made ready for all who might disobey (see Dan. 3:6), so apparently he was expecting some rebellion from some of the officials. He was testing the loyalty of all of his officers to his religious system. Remember that the king had not only brought in Jewish young men to be trained, but other young men as well from other countries he had conquered. There were many who were not native Babylonians in very important roles of leadership in his country. He had to know who would be faithful to the whole system including the religious system, so this was the method by which he chose to test his officers.

Fashioned After His Own Image

The image of gold that was constructed was certainly a great display of wealth and workmanship for that day. Some think that Nebuchadnezzar constructed this image in memory of his father, Nabopolassar.

Others are convinced that he made it an image of Bel, the pagan god of Babylon. Still others believe that he made the image to resemble himself, because of the golden head Daniel had told him about, which represented Nebuchadnezzar in his dream (see Dan. 2:38). In any case we know the statue was large for it was described to be 60 cubits high (90 feet) and 6 cubits wide (9 feet).

In addition, the statue is described as being made of gold, but it is felt that probably a wooden frame was carved and then gold-plated. Yet this was still an extremely valuable piece of workmanship. The statue was put on a flat and expansive plain, and it enabled a great multitude to assemble to worship the image. It was placed on the plain of Dura not far from ancient Babylon. Babylon itself was a city of skyscrapers in that day, yet the height of the image made it visible to great multitudes. In 1854 the archeologist Julius Oppert found a large brick square, 45 feet on a side and 20 feet high. He felt this was the foundation of this image.

When the statue was erected, Nebuchadnezzar then gave the order for all of the leaders and government officials to be present for the dedication (see Dan. 3:2). "The brass" were to go back to their individual provinces and cities to sell the project to the people! This was the first step in the brainwashing program to sell the universal worship of all people toward this golden image. As they assembled on the plain of Dura, it must have been an impressive sight to see this huge image. One could compare it to the crowds who gathered to see the Atlas missile on the launching pad at Cape Kennedy.

The king must have then given the signal, for in Daniel 3:4-6 the herald cried aloud and told the people that at the sound of the music they were to fall down and worship the golden image. Those who were unwilling to worship were to be cast into the burning fiery furnace. The bowing was to be done in unison as they heard the music. There was no provision for spontaneous and personal religion; it was a mob psychology that Nebuchadnezzar had planned. The music was to appeal to the ear and add to the fleshly emotion of the moment to force the people to want to worship this pagan image. The musical instruments used are interesting because there was such a variety. The cornet was a brass instrument. The flute was a woodwind instrument. The harp was in the string family, and the sackbut was like a trombone. The psaltery was a stringed instrument like a harp, while the dulcimer resembled a drum with strings, played with little hammers.

Music that is truly spiritual is a wonderful aid to the worship of our heavenly Father. The Psalms of David reveal this, for they were songs David wrote to the living God. There are many portions of Scripture in both the Old and New Testaments that urge us to worship God in song. Perhaps your church choir needs you to join in singing praises on Sunday mornings! If you don't have an excellent singing voice you can always sing in your home, your car, in the woods or wherever you are! Do you need to learn some hymns by memory so that you can sing praises to the Lord?

In Daniel 3:7 when the people heard the sound of the music all nations and languages fell down and worshiped the golden image. It was practically unanimous. There may have been many who were not totally convinced in their hearts but they gave no visible evidence of it. They attempted to justify their position of compromise, as so many people do today in the ways of the world.

Idolatry is a perversion of man's longing to know God. Yet God did not leave man without a witness of Himself. The worship of idols is inexcusable. "For the truth about God is known to them instinctively; God has put this knowledge in their hearts. Since earliest times men have seen the earth and sky and all God made, and have known of his existence and great eternal power. So they will have no excuse (when they stand before God at Judgment Day)" (Rom. 1:19,20, *TLB*). "Claiming themselves to be wise without God, they became utter fools instead. And then, instead of worshiping the glorious ever-living God, they took wood and stone and made idols for themselves, carving them to look like mere birds and animals and snakes and puny men" (Rom. 1:22,23, *TLB*). This is what Nebuchadnezzar by his example was teaching his dominions to do.

The Bible warns us to stay away from idols (see Exod. 20:4,5; Acts 17:29, 1 John 5:21). There are many present-day "idols" that keep people from worshiping the Lord Jesus Christ. An example is anything that becomes so valuable in a person's life that it pushes out any room for the worship of the true and living God. An idol of our day probably would not be made of gold or silver, it probably would not be a graven image—it might simply be a hobby, an intellectual pursuit, a desire for materialism or power, or a desire to be beautiful or attractive. Many other things could become idols in our lives. None of these things are all wrong in themselves. They become wrong and are condemned by God when they force God out of our lives and take up our time and energy leaving no time for the worship and pursuit of fellowship with the Lord Jesus Christ.

Look very carefully at your own life and see if you find any idols which are more important in your life than your worship of the Lord Jesus Christ. The following is a good Psalm to pray: "Search me, O God, and know my heart: try me, and know my thoughts: and see if there by any wicked way in me, and lead me in the way everlasting" (Ps. 139:23,24, *KJV*).

Not only can we have idols that destroy our relationship with

Jesus Christ, but we can harm our children, grandchildren and even our great-grandchildren by our attitudes and choices in our everyday life. Our descendents learn from us our standards and convictions for life, and as Exodus 20:5 says: "The iniquity of the fathers upon the children unto the third and fourth generation of them that hate me" (*KJV*). The word *hate* here means to ignore and to leave God out of your life. Not only will this affect you as a person, but it will affect the future generations of your family as they "catch your attitudes."

As we think on these things a good prayer to pray is the one found in Matthew 12:17-21: "This fulfilled the prophecy of Isaiah concerning him [the Lord Jesus Christ]: 'Look at my servant. See my Chosen One. He is my Beloved, in whom my soul delights. I will put my Spirit upon him, And he will judge the nations. He does not fight nor shout; He does not raise his voice! He does not crush the weak, Or quench the smallest hope; He will end all conflict with his final victory, And his name shall be the hope of all the world!'" (*TLB*). Certainly any present-day idol cannot be the hope of the world; it cannot bring happiness and give final victory. Only the Chosen One, the Lord Jesus Christ can do this for each person. "God, who is rich in mercy, for his great love wherewith he loved us, even when we were dead in sins, hath quickened us together with Christ . . . . For by grace are ye saved through faith; and that not of yourselves: it is the gift of God: not of works, lest any man should boast" (Eph. 2:4,5,8,9, *KJV*). Have you received the Lord Jesus Christ as your Lord and Savior? Is He your hope and victory? Are you sharing His hope and His victory with the world, which is discouraged and desolate and in a state of turmoil?

Courage to Stand for the Lord Daniel 3:8-12

Apparently the king had appointed certain trustworthy Chaldeans to note any irregularity in the service and report to him. We might ask the question, "Why didn't Shadrach, Meshach and Abed-nego just stay at home during this service of worship of the idol?" It must have been because they would obey the king's orders as far as they could, and at the same time they would bear public testimony against this gross idolatry! This took courage that only the Lord could have given them. Humanly speaking we can imagine our whole bodies trembling amid this vast crowd as we stood for the Lord while everyone else bowed to the idol! Yet these three youths stood unafraid and with great courage knowing that they were being watched and that their actions would be reported to the king (see Ezek. 2:6; 1 Cor. 16:13; Phil. 1:27). "For God hath not given us the spirit of fear; but of power, and of love, and of a sound mind" (2 Tim. 1:7, *KJV*).

When Constantius, the father of Constantine, came to the throne, there were many Christians in public office. He issued an edict requiring them to forsake their faith or give up their places of trust in his realm. Most of them immediately gave up their employment in order to preserve a good conscience. But a few cringed and renounced Christianity. When the emperor had thus tested them, he dismissed everyone who had complied with his stern order, and took all the Christians back again! He accounted for his strange conduct by saying, "It is my firm belief that those who would not be true to Christ would not be true to me!" How the saints of God rejoiced, for not only had they brought honor to the Lord by their actions, but they also had gained stature in the eyes of Constantius.

Through their faithfulness they brought honor to God and promotion to themselves.

The three youths faced a similar test of their faith. They were told to bow down before the golden image that Nebuchadnezzar had set up as an object of worship. Although everyone else obeyed, they refused to sacrifice their spiritual principles on the altar of expediency. Even when threatened with death in a fiery furnace they stood their ground! With God's help and grace they came through the terrible ordeal unharmed. As a result of their faithfulness they brought honor to God and promotion to themselves (see Dan. 3:28-30). Are you a spineless, timid, wavering Christian, or does the world know that you have taken a firm stand on the side of God and truth? Someone has said, "When faithfulness is the most difficult, it is then the most necessary!"

Would You Bow to an Idol? Daniel 3:13-18

Shadrach, Meshach and Abed-nego were really put on the spot by Nebuchadnezzar in Daniel 3:14. He asked them if the charges were true. He asked them if they had refused to worship his gods and the image that he had set up! Then he gave them an opportunity to change their minds and fall down before the image. Nebuchadnezzar again reminded the three of the penalty for refusal—the fiery furnace. In Daniel 3:13 we discover that Nebuchadnezzar fell into great rage and fury when he heard that these men had not bowed down. He asked, "Who is that God that shall deliver you out of my hands?" (Dan. 3:15, *KJV*).

It is interesting to contrast the true devotion of the three young men to God and how their spirits were calm, quiet and meek as they stood before the king. Then compare this to the rage and fury of King Nebuchadnezzar who is superstitious and devoted to false gods. This had turned him into a brute. He must have wondered at the faithfulness of God's servants to the God in heaven.

Shadrach, Meshach and Abed-nego answered the king by saying, "We are not careful to answer thee in this matter" (Dan. 3:16, *KJV*). They failed to use the stilted form of address "O King, live forever." "We are not careful" means that they have carefully weighed the consequences for refusing to obey the king. They are not being careful in giving an answer. In contrast, the wise men who could not give to Nebuchadnezzar the interpretation of his dream of chapter 2 were careful. They stalled for time. However, these three would not hedge or evade the question. They refused to worship an idol. Their reasons were based on the first and the second commandments (see Exod. 20:3-6).

They gave Nebuchadnezzar an answer to his question, "Who is that God who shall deliver you out of my hands?" He had already forgotten what he himself had said in Daniel 2:47. He had told Daniel that his God was "a God of gods, and a Lord of kings." Proud men are still ready to say as Nebuchadnezzar said, "Who is the Lord, that I should fear His power?" The youths gave Nebuchadnezzar a twofold answer to his question: (1) God is able to deliver us! They worshiped the God of heaven and there is no act of power that God cannot do; (2) He will deliver us. They had been given the faith to believe that God would deliver in this emergency. It is one thing to say that God can do a certain thing; it is another thing to say that He will do it!

If God be for us, we don't need to fear what man can do to us.

Regardless of the outcome, these three had purposed to serve God. In this attitude they were solemnly declaring God's sovereign control over the course of human history. They knew that if God did not deliver them out of the fiery furnace, He would certainly deliver them out of the hand of Nebuchadnezzar. They knew that the king could only torment and kill their body and after that there was no more that he could do! Such thoughts will help us when we are suffering and carry us through. If God be for us, we don't need to fear what man can do to us; let him do his worst! God will deliver us either from death or in death into His presence (see Rom. 14:8; 1 Cor. 15:21,22,26,55-57; Phil. 1:21). "Fear not them which kill the body, but are not able to kill the soul" (Matt. 10:28, *KJV*).

The Lord still permits trials and temptations to enter the lives of His children, the Christians. The challenge may come as a temptation to gratify the lusts of the flesh, or as a series of disheartening circumstances. Whatever form the temptation assumes you must not yield, or you will experience spiritual defeat. However, overcoming the temptation will strengthen you and enable you to reach a new plateau in your Christian life. "Therefore, my beloved brethren, be ye steadfast, unmovable, always abounding in the work of the Lord, forasmuch as ye know that your labor is not in vain in the Lord" (1 Cor. 15:58, *KJV*).

A gem cannot be polished without friction, nor a Christian perfected without trial! What about your present suffering? Suppose you have a physical, mental or financial affliction. You may seem crushed by it. Remember that deliverance is possible now, but ultimately it is absolutely certain!

Cast into the Fires of Life Daniel 3:19-27

Nebuchadnezzar reacted quickly and drastically to the response of the three young men by commanding that the furnace be heated seven times hotter than it already was! We can imagine that the servants hurried off to apply more fuel and a forced draft. Next, the king ordered his mightiest men to bind the three captives and cast them into the furnace. They were not even permitted to remove their fine uniforms in which they had come that day! In other words, urgency was of prime importance.

After binding the men, these mighty soldiers carried them off to the furnace. The furnace was so hot that as they threw the bound men into it, the soldiers flamed into burning torches and were killed. Yet, inside where the fire blazed, the three young Jews remained in perfect condition!

The king must have been greatly startled and disturbed that his men had been killed, but he was even more amazed when he drew near the furnace and saw a scene he could not believe! Apparently it was an open furnace that he could look into. He had probably followed the soldiers and took a seat where he could see within the furnace and feel the satisfaction of seeing these three Jewish rebels die. What he saw was not satisfying. He asked his counsellors standing by, "Did not we cast three men bound into the midst of the fire?" (Dan. 3:24, *KJV*). And when they all agreed that they had, in amazement the king said, "I see four men loose, walking in the midst of the fire, and they have no hurt" (v.25). Now Nebuchadnezzar went near the furnace, at least as near as the heat would permit, and called for the men to come out. Actually this call voiced his admission that he had lost. He had defied any god to save these men and now one had! He called them "servants of the most high God" (v.26) and by this was man enough to admit that God had delivered them from death.

The three of them did come out, and before all of the witnesses who had gathered together, they gave the amazing testimony of God's protection by their appearance (see Dan. 3:27). Their bodies had not been touched by the fire; their hair on their head was not singed; their clothes were exactly as they had been before they were bound; and there wasn't even the smell of the fire upon their bodies or their clothes! This was a clear cut miracle!

The witnesses to this miracle would go back all across the empire and would be firsthand witnesses to tell of the miracle they had seen performed by the Jewish God of heaven. Nebuchadnezzar had called them to give praise to the gods of Babylon, but they would go home to tell the story! Many probably gave praise to the God whom Nebuchadnezzar had tried to defy, the God of heaven!

No Other Gods! Daniel 3:28-30

In Daniel 3:28-30 we find a commendable reaction by King Nebuchadnezzar. First of all, he did not try to claim there was any trickery used to protect these three young Jews when they were thrown into the furnace. His first statement was, "Blessed be the God of Shadrach, Meshach and Abed-nego, who hath sent his angel, and delivered his servants who trusted in him, and have changed the king's word, and yielded their bodies, that they might not serve nor worship any god, except their own God" (Dan. 3:28, *KJV*).

The fourth person in the fiery furnace mentioned in Daniel 3:25 as "like the Son of God" (*KJV*) and in Daniel 3:28 as "his angel," in the original text is translated "like a divine being." This person may indeed have been the preincarnate Son of God, Jesus Christ. But if so, Nebuchadnezzar did not know who He was. Angels are called "sons of God" (see Job 38:7). Some think this was the eternal Son of God, the Lord Jesus Christ, the angel of the Covenant, and not a created angel. He did appear often in the Old Testament before He assumed His incarnation as written in the New Testament and therefore it is possible that it could have been the eternal Son of God in the furnace (see Exod. 3:2; 14:19; 32:34; Judges 2:1; 13:6; 2 Sam. 14:17-20; Isa. 6:3-9; and Acts 7:30,35).

GRACE to You!

If you have asked the Lord Jesus Christ to use you as a witness to His grace (God's Riches At Christ's Expense), think it not strange concerning the fiery trial which is sent by Him to mold and prepare you for such work. The three friends of Daniel in Nebuchadnezzar's furnace were not hurt by its flames! They lost only their bonds! They emerged from their ordeal as heroes of faith! They brought added glory to God and were promoted to higher service (see Dan. 3:28-30). You too can find in your present extremity many God-given opportunities. Remember, the Lord often chooses His best workers in the crucible of affliction. "Suffering is the fire by which radiant saints are fashioned and through which God's glory blazes"—Corzine.

While there was nothing personal in Nebuchadnezzar's expression about the God of these young Jewish men, he recognized God's power in delivering them. He granted that their God was superior to his! He did not have a personal experience with Him, though he had been impressed with what he had seen. He acknowledged that God alone gave deliverance. Again, Shadrach, Meshach and Abed-nego are back in Nebuchadnezzar's favor. The king said that anyone who spoke against their God would be severely punished (see Dan. 3:29) and then promoted these three young men in the province of Babylon. Twice now they have had a sentence of death upon them; twice they have been miraculously delivered; and twice they have been promoted! The Lord Jesus Christ is able to keep His own in the world (see Dan. 1:12-15; 2:49; 3:20-30).

GOD'S KINGDOM IS EVERLASTING

DANIEL 4

Before you begin your study this week:
1. Pray and ask God to speak to you through His Holy Spirit each day.
2. Use only your Bible for your answers.
3. Write your answers and the verses you have used.
4. Challenge questions are for those who have the time and wish to do them.
5. Personal questions are to be shared with your study group only if you wish to share.
6. As you study, look for a verse to memorize this week. Write it down, carry it with you, tack it to your bulletin board, tape it to the dashboard of your car. Make a real effort to learn the verse and its reference.

FIRST DAY: Read all of Daniel 4 concentrating on verses 1-3.

1. What does Nebuchadnezzar say the "Most High God" has done for him in these verses? Give verses.

2. **Challenge:** The king realized that his kingdom would only last a limited time, but that God's kingdom is everlasting. There are multitudes of verses throughout all the Scriptures about God's kingdom. What do the following verses say about God's kingdom?

Psalm 22:27,28

Psalm 47:8

Isaiah 9:6,7

3. (Personal) What challenging or encouraging thought about God's kingdom did you find as you read the above verses?

4. Daniel 4:3 speaks of God's "wonders" and "signs." Read Psalm 77:12-19. Pick out the outstanding verses that impress you with the majesty or the wonders of God.

5 a. What did Nebuchadnezzar wish for all men of every language and nation on the earth in Daniel 4:1?

b. What does God the Father and the Lord Jesus Christ give the Christian according to Galatians 1:3?

6. (Personal) Do you have the peace that God wants to give you? (see 2 Thess. 3:16).

SECOND DAY: Read Daniel 4:4-18.

1. What did the king have that alarmed him? Where was he at this time? Whom did he first call for help?

2. Who was the last person the king called in to tell about his dream? Who did the king say this person had in him?

3 a. The king realized that there was something different about Daniel. He had a special quality and discernment, which the king felt "some god" had given him by a "spirit." We know that the Holy Spirit came upon men in the Old Testament at special times to empower them and give them special wisdom from God. What does Exodus 31:1-3 say the Lord gave Bezaleel by the Spirit of God?

   b. What comforting promise do you find for yourself in Romans 14:17?

4. **Challenge:** Read the dream that King Nebuchadnezzar tells to Daniel in Daniel 4:10-18. The three probably represents the king and his kingdom. What do you learn about this in:

   Daniel 4:10-12

   Daniel 4:14,15

5. **Challenge:** How does Daniel 4:16 give a hint that King Nebuchadnezzar might go through a period of insanity?

6. Were any of the wise men of the king able to interpret this dream for him? Did he have confidence that Daniel could interpret the dream?

THIRD DAY: Read Daniel 4:19-27.

1. What was Daniel's reaction to what the king told him about his dream? Do you believe his reaction showed on his face?

2. Do you feel the king's remarks to Daniel in Daniel 4:19 show his affection and respect for his Jewish counsellor?

3. The king showed real kindness to Daniel by his comment, even though he was personally perplexed and upset by his dream! As Christians we should think of others' emotions and needs, even when we may have our own problems on our minds. What do the following verses suggest concerning love and consideration for our fellow Christians? Put them into your own words.

   1 Thessalonians 3:12

   1 Peter 3:8

4. (Personal) Which of these verses was a help to you in some situation in your life? Share with someone how God's love, poured through your life by the Holy Spirit, has surprised or brought joy to you and others. Write your response here.

5. Daniel closed his interpretation of the dream by giving the king advice. What was it? Read Daniel 4:20-27. Give verse.

6. When would the "stump" of Nebuchadnezzar's kingdom be restored to him? Give verse.

FOURTH AND FIFTH DAYS: Read Daniel 4:28-37.

1 a. How long did God give Nebuchadnezzar to do what Daniel 4:27 suggested? Give verse.

  b. Who did Nebuchadnezzar say had built Babylon the great, and how did he say this great kingdom had been built?

2 a. What did a voice from heaven say to the king at this point that fulfilled what Daniel had said?

  b. What does 2 Peter 3:9 say that is appropriate to all of the verses from Daniel 4:27-30?

  c. In Daniel 4:32 what did the voice tell the king about his future?

3. **Challenge:** When were these things fulfilled and how did this mighty monarch now look?

4. Daniel 4:33 portrays a sad picture of the king. In the same way a person without the Lord Jesus Christ is in a sad state. What do the following verses say concerning a person who has never recognized and received God?

   2 Chronicles 12:14

   Psalm 10:3

Jeremiah 7:24

Luke 16:15

5 a. The Lord Jesus Christ is always longing and waiting to forgive
and to receive a person into the family of God. Read the following verses concerning this.

Isaiah 1:18

Isaiah 43:25

John 11:25,26

Romans 3:24-26

   b. Which of the above verses was new to you or helped you to
   understand God's forgiveness through Jesus Christ?

   c. (Personal) Have you ever received what Romans 3:24-26 promises? Read Romans 10:9,11 and Revelation 3:20 to help you
   with your decision.

6 a. When King Nebuchadnezzar's reason was restored to him what
statement did he make about the one true God?

b. (Personal) Can you echo the king's statement? Do you have a faith in God's dominion, power and wisdom?

c. What was the memory verse you chose to hide in your heart this week? Remember many around the world would feel privileged to have just one page from the Bible in their homes to read! Use your freedom while you have it. Learn at least one verse a week.

SIXTH DAY: Read all the Notes and look up the Scriptures.

1. What new thought did you find helpful in the Notes?

2. What personal application did you select to apply to your own life this week?

Study Notes

The testimony of Nebuchadnezzar in the introduction, Daniel 4:1-3, really chronologically would fit in best as the conclusion of the chapter. For at the end of the chapter we find Nebuchadnezzar praising God and honoring the King of heaven. He had recognized the truth and justice of God. The first three verses of this chapter expressed Nebuchadnezzar's conviction that Daniel's God is the most high, the only God who gives mighty signs and wonders and has an everlasting kingdom. His statement actually is an outgrowth of the experiences recorded in this chapter.

As Nebuchadnezzar speaks of peace in verse 1 he is not speaking of a peace brought about by military might and enforced by his superior power! Instead he speaks of the peace of heart that comes to a sinner when he knows that he has been accepted by God. It is peace with God. Nebuchadnezzar's peace was restored to him. Compare Daniel 4:27 with Daniel 4:34.

"Therefore having been justified by faith, we have peace with God through our Lord Jesus Christ . . . and we exult in the hope of the glory of God" (Rom. 5:1,2, NASB). Nebuchadnezzar's testimony is very personal as we see in Daniel 4:2: "It has seemed good to me to declare the signs and wonders which the Most High God has done for me" (NASB). God no longer seems to be God of only the three Hebrew young people. The king now testifies to God's signs, wonders and dominion, which could be a testimony of personal acknowledgement. He recognizes that God's rule is above his rule and that God's kingdom is above his. There is also confession and submission in Daniel 4:3, which seems to express that Nebuchadnezzar had had an experience of real faith in the living heavenly God.

The Holy Spirit alone reveals divine truth to the believer.

Nebuchadnezzar cares about his dream and calls in the holy and wise men of Babylon to interpret it (see Dan. 4:4-9). The king started the story by speaking of himself at rest in his house and flourishing in his palace. Everything was going fine for him, but then he had this fearful dream and the thoughts of it distressed him. As a result and according to custom he summoned these men to interpret the dream. These men could have interpreted the dream, for in that day they had many books and formulas for doing so, but they chose not to do this.

Perhaps the dream was symbolically very tragic even according to their formulas and they did not want to give him such information.

The Holy Spirit Alone Reveals God's Truths Daniel 4:9-27

Since Nebuchadnezzar had learned to rely on Daniel, he probably had intended from the beginning to call him in to check the wise men's interpretation of his dreams. Nebuchadnezzar had learned that Daniel was a Spirit-filled man (see Dan. 2:47,48). Daniel had made it clear that God had revealed Nebuchadnezzar's first dream to him. The Holy Spirit alone reveals divine truth to the believer. But as it is written, "Eye hath not seen, nor ear heard, neither have entered into the heart of man, the things which God hath prepared for them that love him. But God hath revealed them unto us by his Spirit: for the Spirit searcheth all things, yea, the deep things of God" (1 Cor. 2:9,10, *KJV*).

Now the king begins to tell Daniel the dream he had while lying on his bed in his palace. Almost 30 years had passed since Daniel was the "master of magicians" (see Dan. 2) and this is probably why the king called him by his Babylonian name, Belteshazzar. The story doesn't give the definite time when the dream occurred, but there are clues that indicate it was near the end of his reign. Daniel was now about 49 years old since in Daniel 2:48 he was somewhere between 18 to 20 years of age when he was appointed the "prefect" over all the wise men of Babylon.

The general outline of Nebuchadnezzar's dream is that he saw a giant tree that could be viewed to the end of all the earth and on it were leaves and fruit that were attractive and provided shade and shelter for both animals and birds. Then he saw a heavenly messenger called a "watcher and a holy one" (see Dan. 4:13) who came down from heaven and called for the tree to be cut down and destroyed except for its stump. The stump was left to be bound with iron and brass and it would stand in the field with the dew falling on it and with the beasts of the earth moving around it. Then the stump was spoken of in a personalized manner that symbolized it to be a human being (see Dan. 4:15,16). The messenger said this man's heart would be changed from a man's heart to that of a beast (indicating insanity), which would continue while "seven times" passed over it (see Dan. 4:16). At the close of the dream, the dream's purpose was stated. It was to show men that the Most High God rules in the kingdom of men and He has charge of deciding who will and will not rule (see Dan. 2:21). Nebuchadnezzar summarized this dream and then asked Daniel to give its interpretation.

At first Daniel was silent as he realized how ominous this dream was. He wished the dream might be for Nebuchadnezzar's enemies rather than for the king (see Dan. 4:18). When the king saw how shocked Daniel was, he was very kind and said to him, "Let not the dream, or the interpretation therefore, trouble thee" (Dan. 4:19, *KJV*). We can sense in Nebuchadnezzar at this moment a tender heart toward Daniel, the one man he probably thought he could trust among all of his wise men.

Do you ever feel discouraged when you read the newspaper, or listen to the local and world news? It would be easy to feel discouraged for the news is filled with stories of war, death, injustices, cruelty, murder and other depressing subjects. In fact one gets the distinct impression that not too many good things are happening in society today. Yet the Christian must remember that God is still in control of this world, and each day that passes moves us one day closer to the Day of the Lord, when He will bring about His final victory. Only then will the world be ruled by a perfect and faultless leader! "Thou shalt judge the people righteously, and govern the nations upon earth" (Ps. 67:4, *KJV*). "God shall judge the righteous and the wicked: for there is a time there for every purpose and for every work" (Eccles. 3:17, *KJV*; see also Nah. 1:3; Isa. 9:6,7; Acts 17:31; Rom. 2:2,5-16).

Christians are commanded to pray for all who are in authority. "First of all, then, I urge that entreaties and prayers, petitions, and thanksgivings be made on behalf of all men, for kings and all who are in authority, in order that we may lead a tranquil and quiet life in all godliness and dignity. This is good and acceptable in the sight of God our Savior, who desires all men to be saved and to come to the knowledge of the truth. For there is one God, and one mediator also between God and men, the man Christ Jesus, who gave Himself as a ransom for all, the testimony borne at the proper time" (1 Tim. 2:1-6, *NASB*; see also Heb. 13:8; 1 Pet. 1:18-21).

When there is unrighteousness and
injustice in government, the believer
has the responsibility to speak out.

Tragically, many of us fail to pray for our local and national government leaders, as well as for all in authority around this world. We don't find it difficult to spend time criticizing what we feel is wrong, yet we aren't willing to make time to pray about the very same issues and the people concerned with them! Christians should pray daily for all those in public office. If you hang your head in shame because of some of the things your government stands for and is doing, wouldn't it be better to bow your head and ask God to help your leaders? We need to recognize that God instituted government for the well being and welfare of mankind. When there is unrighteousness and injustice in government, the believer has the responsibility to speak out. Yet first of all, it is essential that he pray and ask God's wisdom and guidance (see Jer. 10:7,12).

Second, there is no excuse for the Christian to criticize anything until he has full discernment and knowledge of the problem. This means that the Christian must become willing to become informed through every avenue available to him concerning any issue he wishes to speak about. Then the Christian may be used by God to bring about change! Or at least he has tried to in a manner that is pleasing to God.

We are not, of course, to condone sin—neither did Jesus Christ—but so often we don a self-righteous mask and condemn the sinner along with the sin. Unfortunately, one finds that the world is often more understanding and compassionate than we Christians, the representatives of the God of love! We look only at the sin—the black area—rather than the shaded areas of problems in peoples' lives that drive them into actions that to them seemed to be the only way out at the time.

So then, the question comes—why do we condemn and hardly criticize? Isn't it because we really don't want to get involved with the lives and needs of people? It is much easier to brush them off with a denouncement of their particular sin or weakness. Getting involved hurts. This may cause us to care, and to give a little more, to think, and then to help as the Holy Spirit leads us. The Scriptures tell us in Ephesians 4:32, "And be ye kind one to another, tenderhearted, forgiving one another, even as God for Christ's sake hath forgiven you" (KJV).

We have all been shocked by the stories in the newspapers from time to time of people who would stand on a street corner and do nothing when someone in public was attacked or who would hear screams and would not investigate. When asked why, they simply reply, "We don't want to get involved." But we Christians do the same thing! We do not want to get involved, really. Think! What about that one who works next to you, who lives next door or down the street, and one with whom you go shopping—does he (or she) drink too much, eat compulsively, speak of illicit affairs and lead a questionable life? How do you react? Can this needy one talk to you, or is he afraid of a shocked expression, a prim mouth, or a sharp rebuke? Have you ever wondered why the need to do these things has come about in your friend's life? Do you care enough to make a visit to a home, to invite someone for a cup of coffee so you can listen and talk with this person about God's love for them? (see John 3:16).

How different—but how rewarding—to spend time with the invalid, the lonely, the depressed, the neurotic, the one whose conversation may not be stimulating or interesting. The Lord said, when you prepare a banquet, invite those who are not able to invite you back; in that way, we are ministering, not reciprocating (see Matt. 22:8-10). May I challenge you to become involved this year with at least one individual, to put yourself in his place, to really care about his needs and problems; to "bear ye one another's burdens, and so fulfill the law of Christ" (Gal. 6:2, *KJV*). The second challenge is to pray for your government leaders and become an informed, intelligent Christian in this area. Really care and become involved if God leads you to.

Daniel had become involved with a person he really cared about; that person was King Nebuchadnezzar. Daniel could have given a false interpretation of the king's dream, but he cared enough about the king to give the true interpretation, that it might help him to come to full faith in the true God of heaven. Without the understanding of this dream, Nebuchadnezzar could have become a very bitter man and ended up shaking his fists at Daniel and at Daniel's God. Instead, through the interpretation of the dream and the experience of the dream coming true, Nebuchadnezzar seems to express his true faith in the living God at the end of this chapter.

Daniel first made it clear that the great tree represented Nebuchadnezzar and his kingdom (see Dan. 4:20-22). This tree had grown great in the earth with people all over his empire depending on him for their sustenance. Then Daniel said the cutting down of the tree represented a time of trouble for the king. He would become insane and be driven from men to live with the animals of the field. And this condition would continue until the "seven times" mentioned by the heavenly messenger (see Dan. 4:16).

The meaning of the word *time* seems to be "year." By the time that seven years had passed the king would know that God in heaven did rule and give kingdoms to whom He would. Daniel gave a word of hope for the king by telling him that the continuance of the stump in the field meant that Nebuchadnezzar would continue to live during these seven times and that he would then rule again (see Dan. 4:26). Daniel continued with kind and loving advice to the king to break off from his sins and be merciful to the poor (see Dan. 4:27).

In the words of Abraham Lincoln (April 1863): "We have grown in numbers, wealth, and power as no other nation has grown—but we have forgotten God. We have forgotten the gracious hand that pre-

served us in peace, and multiplied and enriched and strengthened us
. . . . We have vainly imagined that all these blessings were produced
by some superior virtue and wisdom of our own." Perhaps these
words are for us today as much as for our forebearers a century ago.
It behooves us then to humble ourselves, to confess our national sins
and to pray for clemency and forgiveness (see 2 Chron. 7:14). "Seek
ye first the kingdom of God, and his righteousness" (Matt. 6:33,
KJV).

Daniel demonstrated true courage as well as love in interpreting
the king's dream correctly, when it meant serious trouble for Nebuchadnezzar. We see his love and concern for the king as he closes
with this advice to be merciful and break off from his sin. Daniel knew
that if Nebuchadnezzar did this, God would show him mercy and
reduce the degree of discipline that the dream had foretold.

Only One King in Charge Daniel 4:28-33

It seems that the reason for Nebuchadnezzar's insanity was that God
knew that he was unusually proud. He thought of himself as the master of his kingdom and in his pride he had also become unresponsive
to the needs of the poor people by showing no mercy to them. He
needed to be humbled. He needed to realize that the God of heaven
was in final charge over all the earth's kingdoms including his own. He
needed to learn to show humility and be more considerate of the poor.
Since the king did not repent of pride, at the end of 12 months as he
was walking on the roof of his royal palace a voice from heaven came
to him—"O king Nebuchadnezzar, to you it is spoken: The kingdom
has departed from you, and you shall be driven from among men, and
your dwelling shall be with the beasts of the field: and you shall be
made to eat grass like an ox; and seven times shall pass over you,
until you have learned that the Most High rules the kingdom of men
and gives it to whom he will" (Dan. 4:31,32, RSV). As soon as these
words were spoken, they were fulfilled and Nebuchadnezzar was
driven from among men and "his body was wet with the dew of
heaven till his hair grew as long as eagles' feathers, and his nails were
like birds' claws" (v.33, RSV)

A King Brought to His Senses Daniel 4:34-37

The type of mental illness the king suffered is known to medical science as "lycanthropy." The person sees himself as an animal and
wants to live like an animal. In the most common form of this insanity
the person imagines himself to be a wolf. Nebuchadnezzar seems to
have seen himself as an ox as he ate grass like an ox (see Dan. 4:33).

The disease is curable and is known to allow the victim sufficient consciousness of self and God to make intelligent prayer possible. It is likely that since he was the king he was placed in a royal forest or on some farm where he could be watched and protected from harm. After all he was still the king of Babylon although temporarily incapacitated. The indication that the stump was found could signify some form of protection that would serve toward the protection of the king while he was in this state for seven years. Perhaps there were guards who cared for him and watched over him during these days of mental helplessness.

Finally at the end of the set time, Nebuchadnezzar was given enough rationality by God to lift his eyes to heaven and voice a prayer of humility (see Dan. 4:34,35). Perhaps this was the reason that God had allowed this whole episode to happen.

Nebuchadnezzar was restored to the rule of his kingdom (see Dan. 4:36), and even more greatness was added to him after his insanity. It would appear that God gave him more power to show Nebuchadnezzar that God gives extra honor to those who properly honor Him.

Seven years was a long time for a kingdom to remain without an active head and the kingdom condition must have been crying out for restoration. It must have been God alone who kept the leaders from seeking a permanent replacement long before the seven-year period elapsed! God simply superintended the situation so that the people waited and the kingdom survived. The means that God used to bring this about were first of all that Nebuchadnezzar had built a strong organization in his government.

As we noted in chapter 2 this is why God designated him as the head of gold in his first dream. He had appointed able men in his government who could carry on for a substantial time without a head man at the helm. The second way in which God worked was through Daniel. Daniel knew exactly how long the insanity would last and Daniel could have communicated this information to other key people urging them to make arrangements as best they could until the seven years had passed. Daniel had the finest reputation for honesty and reliability, so his words would have been followed carefully.

The king praised God in the very last verse of the chapter, which ties in with Daniel 4:1-3. They give the reason for the record of this whole account of his life. "Now, I, Nebuchadnezzar, praise and glorify and honor the King of Heaven, the Judge of all, whose every act is right and good; for he is able to take those who walk proudly and push them into the dust!" (4:37, *TLB*).

Another man who was tumbled from his pinnacle of pride by God was Robert Blatchford, brilliant author of an influential British magazine known for its relentless attack upon the Christian faith. In one of his editorials, Blatchford said, "There is no Heavenly Father watching over us. He is but the baseless shadow of a wistful human dream . . . if God were a God of love, He would not choose to create a world in which hate and pain should have a place." When this man's wife, who was a Christian, died the proud editor suddenly felt his need for God. The man who had openly denied and brazenly defied the Lord now acknowledged his sinfulness, believed in Jesus Christ, and experienced the joy of forgiveness of sin through the Lord Jesus Christ.

God hates all pride, whether it's a Christian's attitude or the defiance of a professing atheist. If you are a Christian, look into your heart and ask God to show you any area where there is pride; ask God for a humble and contrite spirit (see Isa. 57:15; Jas. 4:6,10). If you have not received the Lord Jesus Christ and proudly say that you do not need the Lord, stop and think. You may stubbornly resist God, but you can never escape Him. Someday you will be forced to acknowledge Him. "He shall call to the heavens from above, and to the earth, that he may judge his people . . . . The heavens shall declare his righteousness: for God is judge himself" (Ps. 50:4,6, *KJV*).

Someday you will be forced to acknowledge God, but how much better to believe and receive Him now! "God shall bring every work into judgment, with every secret thing, whether it be good, or whether it be evil" (Eccles. 12:14, *KJV*). Won't you believe on Jesus Christ and then walk humbly with your God? Those who know God will be humble; those who know themselves cannot be proud! "Grace be to you and peace from God the Father, and from our Lord Jesus Christ. Who gave himself for our sins, that he might deliver us from this present evil world, according to the will of God and our Father" (Gal. 1:3,4, *KJV*).

> Ring the bells of heaven! There is joy today,
>   For a soul, returning from the wild!
> See! The Father meets him out upon the way,
>   Welcoming His weary, wandering child![1]

He who has the right to criticize should have the heart to help.

NOTE
1. W.O. Cushing, "Ring the Bells of Heaven." Public domain.

THE HANDWRITING ON THE WALL

DANIEL 5

Before you begin your study this week:
1. Pray and ask God to speak to you through His Holy Spirit each day.
2. Use only your Bible for your answers.
3. Write your answers and the verses you have used.
4. Challenge questions are for those who have the time and wish to do them.
5. Personal questions are to be shared with your study group only if you wish to share.
6. As you study, look for a verse to memorize this week. Write it down, carry it with you, tack it to your bulletin board, tape it to the dashboard of your car. Make a real effort to learn the verse and its reference.

FIRST AND SECOND DAYS: Read all of Daniel 5 concentrating on verses 1-4.

1. What event did the new king of Babylon give in Daniel 5:1, and how many people attended?

2 a. What was Belshazzar reminded of during the feast? They were objects his father, Nebuchadnezzar, brought from the Temple in Jerusalem.

87

b. What did the king, princes, his wives and concubines use these vessels for while at the feast?

c. While drinking wine from the holy vessels that had been used in the worship of God in Jerusalem, they praised gods of gold, silver, brass, iron, wood and stone. What do the following verses tell you about graven images (idols) and the Lord?

Habakkuk 2:18-20

Acts 17:29

3. **Challenge:** Look at Daniel 5:4 again. Can you think of articles of these same substances that people make their "idol gods" out of today? Not that there is anything wrong with these objects, but when people take excessive interest, think more about them, give more money toward purchasing them, and spend more time, energy and thought on them than they do on the Lord Jesus Christ these objects then become idols. Explain why you have listed particular objects, if you wish.

a. Gold: Example—coins

b. Silver: Example—rings

c. Brass: Example—a collection of bells

d. Iron: Example—iron antiques

e. Wood: Example—boat

f. Stone: Example—diamonds

4. Many people look at their idols as security. Security can be taken away or its value can change. God has an unchanging power to meet all of our needs. How do the following verses express this? Add your name to the verses and claim this promise for yourself.

Romans 4:20,21,24

Ephesians 3:19,20

Philippians 4:19

5. (Personal) Which of the verses in this study today was most meaningful to your life? Share if possible with someone. Tell why it helped you. Pray and ask God to forgive you if you have discovered some "idol worship" in your life. Ask forgiveness in the name of the Lord Jesus, and He will cleanse and free you, as you trust in Him.

THIRD DAY: Read Daniel 5:5-12.

1. What happened in Daniel 5:5?

2. Have you ever felt like the king did in Daniel 5:6, perhaps after an accident, or as you stood on the edge of a high cliff, or entered a deep dark cave? How did the king feel?

3. **Challenge:** What can the Christian remember in any frightening situation? Read Psalm 27 and pick out your favorite verses. Please write them down.

4 a. The king didn't have the comfort that a Christian has. After he had been frightened what did he "cry" for in Daniel 5:7?

   b. What did he promise the one who could interpret the writing?

5. Were the wise men able to read the writing or give the interpretation? Give verse please.

6. Who came into the banquet hall? What did she say, and as a result, who was called to the banquet hall to interpret? State briefly.

FOURTH DAY: Read Daniel 5:13-24.

1. What did the king promise Daniel if he could read the writing and interpret it?

2 a. What was Daniel's reply to the offer of all these gifts? Give verse please.

   b. How could 1 Timothy 1:17 be applied to Daniel's reply to the king?

3 a. Challenge: How do the following verses speak of the "glory of the Lord"?

Psalm 19:1,2

Isaiah 58:7,8

Matthew 5:16

Romans 3:23

Romans 6:23

   b. Which was your favorite verse? Why?

4. What characteristic does King Belshazzar have in common with his father, King Nebuchadnezzar? Read Daniel 5:18-22.

5. What terrible sins had Belshazzar committed according to Daniel 5:23?

6. (Personal) Have you glorified God who gave you breath (see Dan. 5:23) by receiving His Son as your Savior? Read 2 Timothy 1:8-10. Are you glorifying God as a Christian by sharing His Son with others? How are you doing this?

FIFTH DAY: Read Daniel 5:25-31.

1. Give the meaning of each word that was written on the wall.

   a. Mene:

   b. Tekel:

   c. Peres:

2. What happened to Daniel in Daniel 5:29?

3. **Challenge:** What do the following verses say about "God's balances and judgments"? Personalize these verses by adding your name to each one.

   Job 31:4-6

   Proverbs 16:2,3

   Hebrews 9:26-28

4 a. (Personal) Which of the verses in question 5 was most challenging to you? Why? Which was the most encouraging?

   b. Review the verse in this lesson that you memorized this week. Write the verse and its reference and keep it along with others you have learned in an accessible place so you can easily review your verses and grow in your spiritual treasure chest.

SIXTH DAY: Read all the Notes and look up the Scriptures.

1. What new thought did you find helpful in the Notes?

2. What personal application did you select to apply to your own life this week?

Study Notes

Nebuchadnezzar's only son, an evil man known as "Evil-Merodach," succeeded him to the throne about 561 B.C. (2 Kings 25:27). He was murdered by Nergalsharezer who had married one of Nebuchadnezzar's daughters. The murderer took Nebuchadnezzar's son's place on the throne in 559 B.C. Later Nergalsharezer was succeeded by his young son who reigned only a few months before he was murdered by Nabonidus, the husband of another daughter of Nebuchadnezzar! Nabonidus was the last ruler of the Babylonian empire and his son, Belshazzar, was co-ruler. Nabonidus spent most of his reign away from the kingdom on foreign expeditions. Both father and son ruled from 553 B.C. until 539 B.C. when Cyrus captured Babylon for the Medo-Persian Empire.

Since King Nabonidus traveled in foreign countries most of the time, he was not in Babylon at the time this event occurred. This is the reason that he is not mentioned. His existence is also implied by one of the rewards that Belshazzar bestowed on Daniel for interpreting the miraculous writing. He made Daniel "third ruler" in the kingdom rather than second (see Dan. 5:29). He could not make him second ruler because he himself was second since his father, Nabonidus, was first in command.

On this particular night Belshazzar was in Babylon feeling secure and indulging in an orgy (see Dan. 5:1). It was called a great feast but it must have been a sensual affair as the presence of women among the men was unusual in the ancient East (see Esther 1:9). Also the king was very daring in drinking wine before thousands. Even at public feasts oriental kings in the Persian times were screened from public sight.

Since a great deal of material was given on alcohol in the first lesson of this series on Daniel we will not spend much time on the subject of alcoholism as a major social problem of our day. However, since this was a king who was drinking, it was interesting to read the headlines some time ago that said, "Starving man could be healthier than rich drinker." The article by Lew Scarr of the Copley News Service pointed out that a heavier drinker could be closer to malnutrition than the starving poor man who does not drink. Dr. Frank L. Iber, professor of medicine at the University of Maryland School of Medicine, said, "Malnutrition almost surely occurs in the person who consumes more than six drinks a day, although the very heavy drinker—the alcoholic—has the most serious problem." Alcohol is a temporary prop for weak men and women. And it became the downfall of the Babylonians under Belshazzar.

A Lavish Feast Before the Fall Daniel 5:1-4

It is difficult for us to understand Belshazzar's arrogance in putting on a lavish feast for a thousand people when the armies of Gobyrus, the Persian general, were in full view of the city! The celebration could have been some anniversary, or in honor of the king's birthday or coronation day, or perhaps to honor some of their idols. Historians say that Cyrus, who was now with his army besieging Babylon, knew of this feast. He assumed that they would be off their guard, buried in sleep and wine, so took this opportunity to attack the city. This made it easy for him to conquer the city! The city wall was 15 miles square, constructed of brick, 300 feet high, and wide enough for 4 chariots to travel abreast around the city wall. It would have been suitable for a modern freeway! Belshazzar had supplies of grain and water to last for years. Thus this banquet could also have been in defiance to the siege of the enemy on the outside, or perhaps the king hoped to build up the morale of those within.

The archeologist Koldeway, who excavated Babylon, found what is probably the very room in which this banquet took place. The room is similar to all that is described about it in the Bible. It measures 165 feet long by 55 feet wide and has plastered walls (see Dan. 5:5). Most of the plaster is now gone, but the remains of the walls still stand several feet high. Especially important is the niche at the middle of one of the longer walls, directly opposite the door of entrance into the room. It is here that the king would have sat, no doubt on a slightly raised platform so that he could be seen by all present.

The feast was very large with one thousand in attendance, although in ancient times in Persia rulers sometimes fed as many as 15,000 at one time! (see Esther 1:5). It was the custom to eat first and then the drinking time arrived. Belshazzar was tasting the wine in Daniel 5:2 when he made the foolish decision to bring in sacred vessels from Jerusalem to be used for this purpose. Nebuchadnezzar had taken these vessels from the Temple in Jerusalem (see Dan. 1:2) but he had never dishonored them. He had actually placed them in his own place of worship among his gods. Belshazzar's actions were sacrilegious and sensual. The tasting of the wine apparently dulled his sense of propriety and judgment.

He probably felt that such valuable drinking containers obviously would add to the luster of his grand occasion. The Bible specifically says that he ordered the gold and silver vessels (see Dan. 5:2). He wanted the finest. These would have been the containers made principally by Solomon (see 1 Kings 7:47-51; 10:21). Belshazzar also probably wanted to dishonor the God of Judah by doing this. This is made evident by his significant words in Daniel 5:3,4. Even the wives and concubines were allowed to drink from them as they toasted their drinks and praised their gods of gold, silver, brass, iron, wood and stone. Belshazzar, knowing of Nebuchadnezzar's earlier humiliation before the God of Judah (see Dan. 5:22), may have determined not to be intimidated. Perhaps he was demonstrating open defiance in this manner to the God of Judah.

Daniel 5:2 refers to Nebuchadnezzar as Belshazzar's father, but this only means that Belshazzar was related to Nebuchadnezzar and could have been the grandson of Nebuchadnezzar through his mother. In those days this term could have meant grandfather as well as father. Belshazzar's father, Nabonidus, was married to one of Nebuchadnezzar's daughters, and this could have been the reason why the term *father* was used here.

One is almost sickened to read of such evil and sensuous action at this banquet. Yet the Bible warns us about such wicked men and tells us their fate. Suppose you were at a county fair and you saw a hog that had won all sorts of prizes. It had blue ribbons, shiny medals and a beautiful garland of green adorning its neck. Would you envy any of those virtually worthless trinkets or the momentary acclaim the animal has been given? Not if you pause long enough to realize that it's simply been fattened up to be led off to the butcher! This is the way it is with an individual who is classified as an evil doer in the Lord's sight. Solomon in writing the book of Proverbs was led by the Holy Spirit to declare similarly, "Let not thine heart envy sinners" (Prov. 23:17, *KJV*), and again, "Fret not thyself because of evil men, neither be thou envious at the wicked" (Prov. 24:19, *KJV*).

In Psalm 37:2 David explained something more about the end results for those who turned themselves away from God. "For they shall soon be cut down like the grass, and wither as the green herb" (*KJV*). If you've recently had anything to do with mowing a lawn, you know that some blades of grass always rise much higher than others. They may even be among the more energetic weeds in the lawn! But when the rotary piece of steel hits, those tallest are cut down to the same level as the smallest! It makes no difference. And amazingly no one can ever put those blades back! No surgery will ever restore them to their previous height and degree of growth! The psalmist tells us so shall the wicked be. Some may be extremely prosperous, others only moderately so. Still others are just striving; they can't get ahead. The degree of wickedness makes absolutely no difference. In any case they will all be cut down equally. For the Bible reminds us, "He that believeth not is condemned already" (John 3:18, *KJV*). Literally, a person condemns himself because he has not believed in the name of the only begotten Son of God, Jesus, the Christ.

Psalm 37:11 reminds us of the way in which believers in Jesus

Christ should live and think, "But the meek shall inherit the earth; and shall delight themselves in the abundance of peace." Dwight L. Moody observed that, "The beginning of greatness is to be little. The exercise of greatness is to be nothing!" You see humility isn't having low thoughts of yourself. The actual fact is, real humility isn't thinking about yourself at all. The word *meek* in Webster's dictionary tells us to be patient under injuries, to be long-suffering. Meekness and humbleness go together in the Christian life. When the Lord Jesus returns to this earth and makes it worth living in, the words in Psalm 72:7 will be fulfilled, "In his days shall the righteous flourish; and abundance of peace so long as the moon endureth" (*KJV*).

In Daniel 5:4 it was a crowning insult to God as they drank wine from the holy vessels from the Temple of Jerusalem to their gods which were simply idols. Yet today similar situations go on within some churches. A church in Dallas, Texas, in an effort to rise above "Victorian ethics," brought into a Sunday service an exotic dancer. Some churches have hellfire and brimstone, commented the news reporter who described the occasion, but this church has a stripper. The dancer who with her husband is a member of the congregation, kept the worshipers in a fascinated silence as she did the same dance she performs nightly at a Dallas, Texas, "hot spot." When she was through she had left nothing to the congregation's imagination. The minister in speaking of the spiritual value of the performance said: "I don't consider the erotic aspects of the dance wrong. After all, that's the way we all were conceived." From this article we can see that there are people who in the name of worship are just as sensual and unrestrained as they were in Belshazzar's day. They worship false gods just as the Babylonians worshiped false gods.

The Miraculous Writing Daniel 5:5-8

Suddenly amid the drunken orgy, God directly intervened. He did not speak by dream or vision. A hand appeared and wrote on the wall an alarming message which Babylonian wise men could not interpret (see Dan. 5:8). Personally this writer believes it was the writing of the One who later wrote on the sand when the sinful woman was brought to Him by the religious rulers (see John 8:6-12).

The effect upon the king was radical. He was trembling and probably became a sober man. This banquet had been arranged as a morale builder to create courage in the hearts of the Babylonians and now he was completely frustrated. He was so overwhelmed with fear that he could barely stand or speak. Up until this point the dazzling magnificence of the royal banquet had been almost indescribable. Luxurious tapestries probably hung upon the walls. The guests arrived in gorgeous apparel. There were sparkling wines and costly foods, soft lights and sweet music. It all combined to make a pageant to delight the eyes and hearts of the people.

Then as the king was drinking from the sacred vessel, suddenly there appeared fingers of a hand writing on the plaster of the wall, sealing the king's doom and signing his death warrant. God wrote, "God has numbered your kingdom and finished it; you have been weighed in the balances and found wanting; your kingdom is divided and given to the Medes and Persians" (see Dan. 5:26-28). Before the night was over Cyrus had taken the city! In the great light of dawn the streets ran red with blood and Belshazzar's mangled body lay sprawled on the floor of his royal palace at the foot of the golden staircase.

Who Will Decipher the Writing? Daniel 5:9-12

Since the wise men could not interpret the writing on the wall, none of them received the scarlet robe, the gold chain and a third of the kingdom promised to the one who could interpret the writing for him. The language written was unknown to everyone in the room. The queen who entered the room (see Dan. 5:10) must have been an older queen who could have been the wife of Nebuchadnezzar and was probably known as the queen mother. She perhaps arrived as a result of hearing the commotion going on, or was called by someone to the banquet hall. The queen mother could also have been Nitocris, the daughter of Nebuchadnezzar and mother of Belshazzar. Because she referred to Daniel by the introductory phrase "there is a man," it is evident that Daniel no longer held his high position as chief of the wise men. This is understandable as we think of Daniel having served several kings since Nebuchadnezzar. He still held a position in Babylon (see Dan. 8:27) and probably lived not far from the palace so that he could be quickly summoned. Remember, too, that Daniel was 81 years old by now!

The queen mother referred to Daniel as a spirit-filled man, who could decipher the writings. Almost a quarter of a century had passed since the days of Nebuchadnezzar and during this interval Daniel had been retired and set aside. Yet the queen had every confidence that Daniel would interpret the writings. We can hope that she had come to the knowledge of the living, true God.

Trust God for His Gifts Daniel 5:13-24

Although the king had heard of Daniel he had never seen fit to use his services. Now the present emergency forced him to call Daniel from retirement. Belshazzar told Daniel of the failure of his wise men and how he had learned that Daniel could interpret such matters as handwriting. He even promised Daniel the same three attractive honors that he had promised the wise men if he could now do what they failed to do (see Dan. 5:16). The king asked with an air of haughtiness, "Art thou that Daniel, who art of the children of captivity?" Since Daniel was a Jew and a captive, the king did not want to be indebted to him if he could help it. He told Daniel that he had heard of him (see Dan. 5:14), that the spirit of the gods was in him and he had sent for him to try him. Strangely enough he promised the same reward that he had promised the other wise men (see Dan. 5:16). Daniel did not want rewards and he was not pleased that it was mentioned. He was not one of those who divined for money. Daniel saw the kingdom in its last gasp and therefore looked with contempt upon any gifts.

Trust God for His gifts and His rewards, which are far greater in comparison to those the world can give!

This can be a lesson to us! We should despise all the gifts and rewards that this world can give as we see by faith its final period hastening on! Let it give its perishing gifts to others. There are better gifts which we have our eyes and hearts upon; let us be helpful in the world; do it all the real service we can and then trust God for His gifts and His rewards, which are far greater in comparison to those the world can give! The world's gifts are mere trash. "Lay not up for yourselves treasures upon earth, where moth and rust doth corrupt, and where thieves break through and steal: but lay up for yourselves treasures in heaven, where neither moth nor rust doth corrupt, and where thieves do not break through nor steal: for where your treasure is, there will your heart be also" (Matt. 6:19-21, *KJV*).

Daniel preached a pointed and powerful sermon to Belshazzar before he interpreted the handwriting (see Dan. 5:18-24). He pointed out that God had given the kingdom to Nebuchadnezzar and that when he had become filled with pride, God humbled him through a tragic episode. Daniel reminded Belshazzar of this humiliating experience. Although Belshazzar was proud and vain, he knew of his grandfather's insanity and yet had not profited from his experience. By the profane use of the vessels of the Temple which were holy, he had mocked God and insulted Him. Knowing the truth of God, he had

99

rejected it. Daniel concludes his sermon by stating that the handwriting was from God whom Belshazzar had ridiculed.

Do You Know God's Handwriting? Daniel 5:25-29

Daniel reads, translates, and then interprets the handwriting. Someone has said that the reason that Daniel had no difficulty in reading it was that he knew "his Father's handwriting." *Mene* is translated "number." *Tekel* is translated "weight." *Peres* is translated "divisions." God had numbered the kingdom and finished it. Babylon had been weighed in the balance and found wanting. The kingdom was to be divided and given to the Medes and Persians (Dan. 5:26-28).

God weighs mankind: "Talk no more so exceeding proudly; let not arrogancy come out of your mouth: for the Lord is a God of knowledge, and by him actions are weighed" (1 Sam. 2:3, *KJV*). Man is deficient in the weight on God's scale.

If the Bible teaches one truth more than another it is this: if nations and individuals persist in their selfish, sinful, God-denying ways, in spite of God's appeals to show love and mercy, a fearful fate awaits them (see Rev. 2,3). King Belshazzar and his leaders were completely unaware of the imminent tragedy and disaster. One moment they were feasting and drinking as if they had forever to enjoy their kingdom. That very night Belshazzar, the king, was slain (see Dan. 5:30). The drift of societies to destruction is so imperceptible that they are at the brink before they know it. "It can't happen here" is a universal superstition and the prelude to the inevitable disaster.

Our nation is in danger of assuming that power is the answer to all problems. The breakdown of moral standards, sexual promiscuity, blatant lawlessness and drug abuse can bring the most proud and powerful nations to their knees in defeat and tragedy. People do not deliberately choose to plunge over into the abyss. They edge toward the precipice little by little, and until they are already falling they aren't aware of the danger. The final disaster always seems like a sudden unexpected affair. Until the very last moment they are feasting without an awareness that the enemy stands at the gate.

The message of the Bible is: "Now is the accepted time; behold, now is the day of salvation" (2 Cor. 6:2, *KJV*). "You know that you were ransomed from the futile ways inherited from your fathers, not with perishable things such as silver or gold, but with the precious blood of Jesus Christ, like that of a lamb without blemish or spot. He was destined before the foundation of the world but was made manifest at the end of the times for your sake. Through him you have confidence in God, who raised him from the dead and gave him glory, so that your faith and hope are in God" (1 Pet. 1:18-21, *RSV*).

Do you have this faith and hope? Are you sharing this great truth with others? The story of King Belshazzar shows us that there is not as much time as we think! We have come to believe that God is not in a hurry and that things will develop automatically and gradually. We assume that it is quite unsophisticated for us to get excited about doing anything immediately! However this message is quite out of tune with the spirit of the Bible which says, "Now is the accepted time: now is the day of salvation."

Intellectual pride and a subtle love of comfort, pleasure and material security can drive God off the throne of your life. If you are not putting God first in everything, then you are breaking the first and greatest commandment; you are guilty of the greatest sin possible against God, greater than murder, adultery or any other sin. If anything in your life rates higher than God and His will for you, then this thing is an idol and you are an idolater. Have you been weighed in the balances and found wanting? Receive by faith the forgiveness for sin He freely offers and for which He has fully paid. If you do this, then for you there will never be the awful doom and final judgment as that which befell the great but doomed King Belshazzar of Babylon.

God's Kingdom Is Coming Daniel 5:30,31

At the very time of the banquet, the Medes were marching underneath the walls of Babylon where the river had flowed. They had diverted the river's flow! While most of the Babylonians were in bed, the river had left its bed to make room for thousands of marching feet. Xenophon, the Greek historian, records for secular history the account of the way in which the Persians took the city. Belshazzar was slain and Darius, the Median, was now the ruler of the kingdom of silver (see Dan. 2:32). Details of this siege and fall of Babylon had been prophesied long before by Jeremiah (chapters 50,51). God also fulfilled Isaiah's prophecy regarding Cyrus (see Isa. 44:24-28; 45).

Darius, the Mede, took the kingdom in partnership with and by consent of Cyrus who had conquered it. They were partners in war and conquest and so they were as rulers. Darius was approximately 62 years old, which was the reason Cyrus, his nephew, gave him the precedence. The story of the fall of Babylon has been found in four separate sources of historical accounts (Herodotus, Xenophon of the fifth and fourth centuries B.C. respectively, and the cuneiform records of both Nabonidus and Cyrus). Not only that, this conquest fulfilled the dream which Nebuchadnezzar had been given by God and Daniel had interpreted in Daniel 2:31-45. History proves the Bible to be true.

Finally, as we consider the rise and fall of governments, we have that wonderful hope that "In the days of these kings shall the God of heaven set up a kingdom, which shall never be destroyed: and the kingdom shall not be left to other people, but it shall break in pieces and consume all these kingdoms, and it shall stand for ever" (Dan. 2:44, *KJV*). This is the kingdom that the Lord Jesus Christ shall reign and rule over. It will be a kingdom of righteousness, peace and joy! How wonderful it is to be a Christian and realize that God is in control of world affairs and will one day set up the perfect kingdom on earth! Do you have peace and joy from the Lord Jesus Christ as you look forward to that day? (see John 3:16-18; Rev. 3:20).

DOOMED OR DELIVERED?

DANIEL 6

Before you begin your study this week:

1. Pray and ask God to speak to you through His Holy Spirit each day.
2. Use only your Bible for your answers.
3. Write your answers and the verses you have used.
4. Challenge questions are for those who have the time and wish to do them.
5. Personal questions are to be shared with your study group only if you wish to share.
6. As you study, look for a verse to memorize this week. Write it down, carry it with you, tack it to your bulletin board, tape it to the dashboard of your car. Make a real effort to learn the verse and its reference.

FIRST AND SECOND DAYS: Read all of Daniel 6 concentrating on verses 1-9.

1. What would have been Daniel's work as one of the three top presidents selected by Darius, who was now king of Babylon?

2. **Challenge:** What was unusual about Daniel holding this new high position in the Medo-Persian Empire? Review Daniel 1:18-20; 2:46-49; 4:18; 5:17,29-31.

3 a. What do you learn about Daniel in Daniel 6:3? Should this be true of a Christian who is in business, or of a homemaker who is working in some organization?

   b. The following verses are guidelines for the Christian to live by in every area of life so that respect, honesty and honor will be qualities in his or her life, as they were also in Daniel's life and work. Put these verses into your own words.

   Proverbs 22:29

   Romans 12:11,12

4 a. Where did Daniel's enemies first look for some accusation against him. Did they find any fault with him? (see Dan. 6:1-9).

   b. Next, how did these men plan to find a fault in Daniel so they could "be rid of him" in the government? Give verse.

5 a. Who gathered together to take a decree to King Darius that would "trap" Daniel concerning obedience to his God?

   b. How was the decree worded by these influential men of high office? How did they appeal to the pride of King Darius, so that he would make a quick decision with no thought about the results of such a decree? Give verse.

c. Was King Darius's ego impressed enough by this approach that he responded quickly to the appeal?

6 a. What should a proper attitude be toward flattery? Do men and women plot in just such a manner today to gain what they want? Give illustrations without using names. What does Proverbs 26:28 say about flattery?

b. If you are in a similar situation to Daniel's, there is a prayer in Psalm 5 you can read and make your own right now. Especially note verses 11, 12 and write them down here.

THIRD DAY: Read Daniel 6:10-15.

1 a. Where had Daniel always prayed and how often did he pray? Did the decree King Darius signed stop Daniel's prayers to God?

b. What position did Daniel take when he prayed, and what two things did his prayers consist of that ours should also contain today?

c. (Personal) Which of the two elements of Daniel's prayer do you feel you need to have more of in your prayer time: asking or praising? Why not make a list of what has been lacking in your prayers to remind you to include these things?

2. Psalm 3 could probably have been incorporated into Daniel's first prayer after he heard that the decree was signed that no man could pray to any God for 30 days. Read this Psalm and divide it into *prayer* and *praise*, as you feel it should be done. Answers will vary, so don't be afraid to try it! You may shorten and use your own words if you wish.

PRAYER: Example—V. 1. Many trouble me and rise up against me.

PRAISE: Example—V. 3. But thou, O Lord, art my shield of defense, my glory and you uplift my spirit.

3. Who do you think the men were who came, listened and watched Daniel pray? (see Dan. 6).

4 a. Like tattling children, who did they go to and what did they tell this person about Daniel? Give verse.

   b. **Challenge:** Do you sense any racial prejudice in the way these men made their statement concerning Daniel in Daniel 6:13?

5 a. Racial prejudice has always been a problem throughout all world history. What do Malachi 2:10 and Genesis 3:20 remind you about God's creation of man?

b. As each one of us thinks about our own racial prejudices, whatever their causes may be, let us read and put down in our own words what God led Paul to write concerning honoring a fellow human being in a Christlike way. Read Philippians 2:3,4 and put it down in your own words including your name.

6. How did the king feel when these men who had spied on Daniel reported that he was continuing to pray despite the petition he had signed? Does this give you any indication of the respect the king had for Daniel? (see Dan. 6:14,15).

FOURTH DAY: Read Daniel 6:16-23.

1 a. After reading Daniel 6:16 do you believe that Daniel had been witnessing to King Darius about his God?

b. (Personal) Certainly Daniel had not let Darius's high position stop him from sharing his faith in the heavenly Father. Do you have excuses you use when the Holy Spirit provides opportunities for you to speak out about your faith? What are ways you can or have shared your faith with a:

Child:

Neighbor:

Business associate:

Relative:

Stranger:

2 a. How was Daniel enclosed in the lions' den? Was there any chance he could have been smuggled out to safety?

   b. How did the king spend the night while Daniel was in the lions' den? How does this show his great respect and affection for Daniel?

3 a. What was the first thing the king did early in the morning? What did he call out?

   b. How exciting it must have been to have heard Daniel's victorious reply! How did he tell the king that the living God had delivered him?

4 a. How did Daniel appear when they brought him out?

   b. Why was Daniel kept safely through the night, according to Daniel 6:23?

5. We know that some Christians suffer, are persecuted for their faith and sometimes become ill. But God chose to protect Daniel, as a witness to His great power as the one true God. God was a shield and defender to Daniel in the lions' den. He sent His angel to defend Daniel (see Dan. 6:22). When Christ was arrested what did

He say about angels? (see Matt. 26:53). Yet He chose to die for our sins instead of having angels rescue Him.

6. **Challenge:** Look up other verses on angels in your concordance and share your favorites with your study group or with some person. If you don't have a concordance in your Bible, look up the word *angel* in the dictionary and share this definition.

FIFTH DAY: Read Daniel 6:24-28.

1 a. What gruesome order did the king give concerning the men who had accused Daniel?

b. Who else had to suffer as a result of these men's sin of jealousy and plotting against Daniel?

2. **Challenge:** Do you believe that families and children today may suffer as a result of others' sins? Give some specific examples without naming any person by name.

3. (Personal) What could you do for someone who is suffering because of a lack of attention and love or is hurting in some other way? (see John 15:4,5,8,12).

4. **Challenge:** How would you characterize Darius's thinking about Daniel's God, who saved Daniel from death? Give verses.

5. What happened to Daniel according to Daniel 6:28?

6. Review the verse in this lesson that you memorized this week. Write the verse and its reference and keep it along with others you have learned in an accessible place so you can easily review your verses and grow in your spiritual treasure chest.

SIXTH DAY: Read all the Notes and look up the Scriptures.

1. What new thought did you find helpful in the Notes?

2. What personal application did you select to apply to your own life this week?

Study Notes

The story of Daniel in the lions' den is one of the most familiar chapters in the book of Daniel, and concludes the strictly historical section of the book. It tells of God's miraculous deliverance of Daniel from the mouths of hungry lions. This is another illustration of the keeping power of God, and is a counterpart of chapter 3 where God preserved the three friends of Daniel in the fiery furnace.

Babylonia was in control of the country up to this point. Now it is controlled by the Medes and the Persians. The exact length of time since the fall of Babylon cannot be determined, but at least a few months have elapsed. Amazingly enough Daniel was included in the newly established regime.

The identity of Darius has long been questioned. In Daniel 5:31 we learn that he is 62 years old, but history tells us of no man named Darius who ruled at this time over Babylon. Cyrus, according to Daniel 1:21 and 10:1, was the Persian king in supreme authority at this time (see Isa. 44:28; 45; 2 Chron. 36:22,23; Ezra 1:1-4). Secular historians and archeological evidences testify to Cyrus's authority. The truth of the story may stand, however, since Darius obviously was a "sub king" under Cyrus. He was a local "king" over the realm of the Chaldeans (see Dan. 9:1).

There are three principles used that have been set forth by scholars: (1) Darius was Cyrus himself under a different name here in the book of Daniel; (2) Darius was Cambyses, the son of Cyrus, who later became Cyrus' full successor but could have served temporarily as ruler only of Babylonia; (3) He was one named Gubaru in secular sources, and is known to have been appointed governor over Babylonia by Cyrus immediately after the fall of the city.

A good case has been made for Gubaru in a book by John Whitcomb called *Darius the Mede*. We do know that it was common for kings in that day to have two or more names. In faith we can wait for further information when we stand before God in heaven.

And so this chapter begins with Babylon, the head of gold, having been removed from the number one spot as a world power. In its place the Medio-Persian Empire, represented by the arms of silver ruled (see Dan. 2:32). Daniel bridged the gap between these two world powers by holding high positions in both. In the Babylonian Empire he had the office similar to what we would call a prime minister today. In the Mede empire he held perhaps his most important post since he had been reduced to obscurity during the last days of the Babylonian Empire. Darius placed him in a position of great power.

There's Value in Old Age Daniel 6:1-9

Darius was a wise ruler and did not try to do all of the governing himself. He appointed 120 princes and 3 presidents to help him reign over the dominion of Babylon (see Dan. 6:1,2). The presidents were like overseers and the princes had to give an account to them. This was probably to keep the princes from stealing from the government!

Daniel, known for his integrity, had over 50 years of public service behind him, and therefore was a prominent figure in Babylon. This is probably why he was preferred above the other presidents (see Dan. 6:3). And the king considered setting him over the whole realm. This was most unusual since he was a holdover from the enemy administration! This suggests the value of age in positions of great responsibility and also the integrity of a believer in God. His appointment can only be explained on the basis of God's direct superintendance! Of course his reputation for being able to interpret such matters as miraculous writing certainly came to Darius's ears. Also the known fact that Cyrus followed the general policy of peaceful transition from one government to the next played a part in Daniel's appointment.

Proverbs 16:19-23 seems to characterize what Daniel's life must have been like, "Better poor and humble than proud and rich. God blesses those who obey him; happy the man who puts his trust in the Lord. The wise man is known by his common sense, and a pleasant teacher is the best. Wisdom is a fountain of life to those possessing it, but a fool's burden is his folly. From a wise mind comes a careful and persuasive speech" (*TLB*).

Today, society often does not feel that a person is useful in his or her old age. How untrue it is when a person is totally committed to God and wants to be of service to Him. Daniel was a perfect example of this! Daniel lived a life of total-faith commitment to God. This is why God could use him all of his life.

> *If you are a child of God you ought to live so that the charges that will inevitably be leveled against you will be a lie!*

The story in Daniel 6 moves on as a treacherous plot is formed by the other two presidents and at least some of the princes under them (see Dan. 6:4,5). They wanted to find something by which to accuse Daniel so that the king would have to punish him rather than elevate him. From their statement in Daniel 6:4 we discover that they could find no fault in Daniel. He was faithful and had not committed any act to discredit himself. His life was above reproach. He was faithful and loyal to his office and to God.

All Christians Are Under Pressure

Every Christian is under the same pressures that Daniel faced. If you are a child of God you ought to live so that the charges that will inevitably be leveled against you will be a lie! You cannot keep people from talking about you or trying to blame you for things, but you can live so that they cannot find any fault in you by the power of the Holy Spirit. "In everything you do, stay away from complaining and arguing, so that no one can speak a word of blame against you. You are to live clean, innocent lives as children of God in a dark world full of people who are crooked and stubborn. Shine out among them like beacon lights, holding out to them the Word of Life, [Jesus Christ]" (Phil. 2:14-16, *TLB*).

Daniel had probably practiced his prayer life as long as he had resided in Babylon. He had never forgotten God. God had made him a man of integrity and had given him great power and honor. He took time, three times each day to spend with God in silence of prayer. As we think of our busy world today with all of its many noises, we realize that silence hath charm. Picture, if you will, some solar ray suddenly causing all radios, cassette players, stereo sets and televisions to stop working. Trembling hands impatiently twirl dials and adjust knobs, flip switches. Eyes are dilated with fear! Breathing comes in spasms!

Marx was wrong. Religion isn't the opiate of modern man. Incessant sound is! We will listen to anything to avoid silence—long, pointless talk shows, boring conversations, 'round the clock news, rock and country music. We like sound because it blocks off the despairing cry of our own souls as well as the still small voice of God. We need occasionally to take God's hand and journey into the fearful land of silence. It can be both painful and healing with the presence of the One who is able to still the despairing cry and give us a new song of thanks. Yes, silence hath charm! Will you take time today to discover this charm as you take God's hand and journey in prayer with Him?

These evil presidents and princes made a plan to get rid of Daniel by taking advantage of Darius's vanity. He easily yielded to flattery so these men, knowing his weakness, appealed to it. They decided on a course of action involving Daniel's faithfulness to his God. This was really a compliment to Daniel as they were impressed by his religious faithfulness and believed that they could build a plot against him based on it. They drafted a bill, gave it unanimous approval, and passed it on to the king that he might make it a law (see Dan. 6:7-8). The bill gave Darius the position of a god—for prayer could be offered only to him for the next 30 days. Anyone who disobeyed this law would be cast into the den of lions (see Dan. 6:7). These men lied when they said, "All the presidents of the kingdom have agreed to this decree" (see Dan. 6:7), for obviously Daniel had not agreed and never would have to such a decree.

Prayer should rise spontaneously from our hearts at any moment of need; but it also should be a practice for us to take a certain time during each day to pray.

Darius displayed his vanity. He felt flattered by this remarkable honor and foolishly signed the decree (see Dan. 6:8). According to the law of the Medes and the Persians anything signed by the king could not be changed. If only he had waited he might have made some inquiry that would have revealed the plot involved but he acted impulsively. How often we as Christians are sorry when we act impulsively without stopping to consult the Lord about a decision! We, too, are guilty of vanity. "For the Lord loves justice and fairness; he will never abandon his people. They will be kept safe forever; but all who love wickedness shall perish. The godly shall be firmly planted in the land, and live there forever. The godly man is a good counselor because he is just and fair and knows right from wrong" (Ps. 37:28-31, *TLB*).

Are You Disciplined in Praying? Daniel 6:10-15

Now we see one of Scripture's outstanding examples of obedience to God as word came to Daniel about the decree. He quickly recognized the plot behind it. He did not act foolheartedly. Boldly opening his windows he went ahead and prayed. He did not act in a cowardly and compromising manner. Actually Daniel was obeying God as he prayed facing Jerusalem. Solomon had given this procedure in his dedicatory prayer of the Temple (see 1 Kings 8:44-48; 2 Chron. 6:36-39). Today all is changed. No earthly place is preferred above another (see John 4:21-24).

All of his life Daniel had given a strong testimony for his God. He had told people in Babylon how his God could provide for those who trusted in Him. If he should now appear to stop praying to this God, all of his previous testimony would be of no value. People would think that he had not meant what he had said. Daniel undoubtedly felt that the importance of this testimony was much more valuable than the continuance of his life. What a challenge he gives to every Christian!

Daniel knelt and prayed as he had always done. To have maintained such a heavy schedule of governmental responsibilities and still continued the remarkable discipline of prayer life showed just how much Daniel loved his Lord. Now he continued this schedule even in the face of danger. Prayer should rise spontaneously from our hearts at any moment of need; but it also should be a practice for us to take a certain time during each day to pray. It is such a great privilege to talk to God and Daniel knew this privilege three times a day. "But I will call upon the Lord to save me—and he will. I will pray morning, noon, and night, pleading aloud with God; and he will hear and answer. Though the tide of battle runs strongly against me, for so many are fighting me, yet he will rescue me. God himself—God from everlasting ages past—will answer them! For they refuse to fear him or even honor his commands" (Ps. 55:16-19, *TLB*).

The story is told of a little boy who became separated from his mother in New York City and was picked up by an officer who found him crying. The compassionate policeman took the little boy to the station to wait for his mother's call. He assured him that if they had not located her by the time he went off duty at 12 o'clock, he would personally take the boy home. When the little boy stopped crying, he was ushered into the sergeant's office. It was getting dark and they suggested that he should take a nap on their large leather couch.

The little boy hesitated, so the sergeant said, "It's all right, go and lie down. We will be taking you home shortly." The boy did as he was told but seemed so restless that the officer asked him kindly, "What's the matter?"

The little boy asked, "Would you mind if I said my prayers as I do at home?"

The officer replied, "Of course not," although he was somewhat startled by the request. The boy kneeled down by the side of the couch and turning his little face heavenward offered his simple goodnight prayer. Then happy and content he jumped into his "bed away from home" and immediately went to sleep. The officers who had taken off their hats and bowed their heads while the little boy said his prayers were strangely silent. Some of them had tears trickling down their cheeks. This little boy had preached a powerful sermon concerning the influence of a Christian home where prayer is the regular order of the day. What is it like in your home? Are you training your children to take time to talk to God each day? As grandparents and friends of families with little children, are you assisting in this process by sharing good Christian books with suggestions on family devotions

115

with young parents? "Be still, and know that I am God" (Ps. 46:10, *KJV*).

As we return to Daniel, we discover that the enemies of Daniel were spying upon him in order that they might accuse him (see Dan. 6:11). They no doubt knew his time schedule and made sure they were watching him the very first time he prayed following the signing of the decree by the king. After hearing Daniel's prayer these men rushed immediately to the king and reminded him of the decree he had signed and accused Daniel of violating this law. They identified Daniel as "of the children of the captivity of Judea" (Dan. 6:13, *KJV*) thus identifying him as a Jew. Apparently they had an attitude of racial prejudice toward anyone from Judea.

The king tried to get out of this vicious plot (see Dan. 6:14), because he respected and loved Daniel. But since the law could not be changed, the enemies of Daniel were quick to remind the king of this, and he actually was a slave to his own law at this point.

Wait Upon God for His Wisdom Daniel 6:16-28

The king had to put Daniel in the lions' den contrary to the king's own wishes. This den was an underground cave, which was either a natural cave or one that had been dug out of the earth. It had an opening at the top through which the prisoners were let down (see Dan. 6:23). Also there may have been a side entrance through which the lions were let in. This den must have been quite large to have allowed for several lions to move about and also to permit all of the conspirators and their families to be cast into it at one time (see Dan. 6:24).

According to Oriental custom the sentence had to be carried out before the end of the day on which the accusation was made, so Darius gave the order for Daniel to be taken captive (see Dan. 6:16). Daniel was brought to the lions' den. At that moment it would have been easy to think that God had forgotten him. Years before, the same type of experience had happened to his three friends when they faced the fiery furnace. Now it was Daniel's turn and we can assume that he faced the challenge with equal commitment and trust in God.

As a Christian, do you have the strength to suffer wrong in the spirit in which Christ did? "That I may know him, and the power of his resurrection, and the fellowship of his sufferings, being made comformable unto his death" (Phil. 3:10, *KJV*). "I can do all things through Christ which strengtheneth me" (Phil. 4:13, *KJV*). Whether it be some great wrong that is done to you, or some little offense that you meet in daily life, before you fix your thoughts on the person who did it, first be still and remember that God allows you to come into this trouble so you will glorify Him in it. This trial, be it the greatest or least, is allowed by God and is His will concerning you. You must recognize and submit to God's will in it. Then, with God's peace, you will receive wisdom to know how to behave in it.

Is Your Witness Showing?

Daniel was faithful to God. Daniel was a powerful witness as he was taken to the lions' den. Amazingly the king himself was there and tried to console Daniel whom he had sentenced. He told Daniel, "Your God whom you constantly serve will Himself deliver you" (Dan. 6:16, NASB). This amazing statement reveals that Daniel had witnessed to Darius concerning the true God. Daniel had not let Darius's high position stop him from speaking about his faith in the living God.

Daniel was thrown to the hungry lions, a stone cover was set in place and sealed with the official stamps of both the king and his lords to assure the fact that no one could roll back the stone and rescue Daniel during the night. The seal was made of wax or soft clay imprinted with the official stamps. The double stamp was to indicate that the stone could not be moved without the permission of the king and these lesser officials.

In Daniel 6:18 we find how the king felt about Daniel and how disturbed he was by the action he had had to take. He did not eat, he did not want any form of entertainment brought to him and he could not sleep that night. He must have felt very guilty for his part in this whole matter. As a result, as the first light of morning dawned he was dressed and on his way to the den of lions. He called out, "Daniel, servant of the living God, has your God, whom you constantly serve, been able to deliver you from the lions?" (6:20, NASB).

What an unusual situation! A king was standing very early in the morning calling down into a den of lions to the man he had sentenced asking if the man's God had somehow been able to save him, and hoping that it was true! Daniel gave a thrilling response to the question. He told the king that his God had sent an angel that had shut the lions' mouths so that they didn't hurt him. Probably Daniel had slept better in the lions' den than the king had in his royal palace! God had protected Daniel just as He had protected Daniel's three friends in the fiery furnace. They were untouched by the fire and Daniel was unhurt by any of the great beasts.

Another parallel to this story is that Daniel enjoyed the company of an angel during the night just as the three friends had enjoyed a heavenly messenger in the middle of the fiery furnace! Perhaps the angel who ministered was the same one that Nebuchadnezzar had seen in the furnace, "like the son of God." It could have been Christ Jesus Himself (see 2 Tim. 4:17).

The king gave the immediate orders that Daniel be lifted out of the lions' den. There was not even a scratch found upon him (see Dan. 6:23). Why? Because he believed in his God. Daniel was saved by faith. "Who through faith subdued kingdoms, wrought righteousness, obtained promises, stopped the mouths of lions" (Heb. 11:33, *KJV*). Daniel rested in God alone for deliverance. We, too, must rest in God alone for our deliverance.

In Daniel 6:24 the king ordered the accusers and their families to be cast into the lions' den and receive the death that had been intended for Daniel. Again, God's principle had come true: "Whatsoever a man soweth, that shall he also reap" (Gal. 6:7, *KJV*). It is sad to think that the families of these men had to suffer, too, as a result of the sins of their fathers.

Today, there are many families and children who suffer as a result of the sins of their parents. Often innocent families and children suffer as a result of the side effects of such things as divorce, drugs, alcohol, materialism and many other social problems in our day. There are many children who are beaten and actually killed by their parents today. Materialism causes children to suffer a lack of guidance from fathers and mothers who often work just to earn money for the sake of having more money to buy more things. As individual Christians if we know that someone is suffering not because of their own sin, but because of a lack of attention and love, or a sin of some family member, we have a responsibility to help that person. Are you willing to look around and discover people who need your help and love? Will you take up this challenge in your life today?

Darius followed this incident by issuing a decree to all of Babylon that the people were to "tremble and fear before the God of Daniel" (see Dan. 6:25-28) He called Daniel's God the Living God, and said that He is steadfast forever; His kingdom will not be destroyed and He will deliver and rescue as He had just done in delivering Daniel "from the power of the lions." Such a statement from a king whose background was paganism was most remarkable. He made these statements as an official edict for everyone in the land to read. Certainly we hope this suggests a change of heart on his part and we may hope that he had a genuine faith in Daniel's God.

The last verse indicates that Daniel continued to prosper during Darius and Cyrus's rule, which was simultaneous. It was Cyrus who made the decree permitting the Jews to return to Palestine (see 2 Chron. 36:22,23; Ezra 1:11). Perhaps the lions' den experience also influenced Cyrus's life. We can hope that he, too, believed in the One True God. This chapter testifies to God's faithfulness to those who are faithful to Him. May we ever remember to be faithful to our Lord Jesus Christ.